PRAISE FOR *THE STRATEGIC BUSINESS INFLUENCER*

"There's a reason most CEOs struggle to make marketing work: They don't see how their role has changed. This book delivers that clarity—and a strategy that aligns leadership with growth."

—Camille Burns, CEO, Women Presidents Organization

"For anyone looking to elevate their strategic influence and impact, both personally and professionally, this book is a must-read. Paige does a masterful job articulating the 'why' for visibility, in life and in business."

—Kelley Fain, President, Shaw Commercial

"Most branding books are all talk. This one is actually useful. Paige keeps it real and shows leaders how to turn what they are doing into results."

—Brandon Phillips, World Series Champion, 3x MLB All-Star, 4-time Gold Glove Winner, Silver Slugger Award Winner, and Owner, The Atlanta Smoke

"Think you're too busy as a CEO to build your brand? Paige shows how you're already doing it—just not strategically. This book will show you how to amplify your actions to deliver business results."

—Joel Trammell, 5-time CEO, Author, Chairman, Founder, and Investor

"This isn't about likes, followers, or fame. It's about building a company that lasts by leveraging your leadership, your voice, and your mission. Paige nails the modern formula for trust that scales."

—Dr. Kara Hartl, Founder and CEO, Troy Medical

"Most books teach tactics. Paige teaches strategy: how to weave your brand into every message so your company stands out and sustains momentum."

—Sarah Goodman, Managing Partner and President, Eminence M&A Strategies

"This is the book I wish I had when I launched my business. I never saw myself as someone who could 'do sales,' but this book affirms what I had to learn the hard way: Authenticity and honesty aren't just acceptable—they're powerful. For leaders who would rather lead with purpose than self-promote, this book redefines what effective marketing can be."

—Michelle Ray, CEO, Absolute Facility Solutions, LLC

"*The Strategic Business Influencer* marries practical, actionable steps with an unwavering commitment to authenticity as one focuses on branding. I found the book's six-step approach, from defining your unique 'Influence ID' to turbocharging referrals, to be a refreshing road map for leaders who understand that genuine connections and high-touch interactions are the true currency in business and the most enduring asset in a competitive landscape."

—Christa Kleinhans Tuttle, Founder, Investor, Strategic Advisor, Board Facilitator

"Paige gives leaders the blueprint to thrive in today's world. If you're still relying on old-school PR or chasing social media trends, read this before you waste another dollar."

—Jennifer Seay, Founder and CEO, Art + Artisans

"Paige Velasquez Budde is an amazing leader who is able to translate her deep knowledge and breadth of experiences in marketing into this book. This book gets one thing right that most miss: marketing only matters if it leads to business results. Paige makes the case for building trust as a growth strategy—and gives you the framework to make it happen."

—Jane Harvey, President and Owner, Three AlphaGraphics Locations

The
STRATEGIC
BUSINESS
Influencer

BUILDING A BRAND

WITH A SMALL BUDGET

PAIGE VELASQUEZ BUDDE

Matt Holt Books
An Imprint of BenBella Books, Inc.
Dallas, TX

Matt Holt is an imprint of BenBella Books, Inc.
8080 N. Central Expressway
Suite 1700
Dallas, TX 75206
benbellabooks.com
Send feedback to feedback@benbellabooks.com

BenBella and *Matt Holt* are federally registered trademarks.

Printed in the United States of America
10 9 8 7 6 5 4 3 2 1

Library of Congress Control Number: 2025024287
ISBN 9781637747704 (hardcover)
ISBN 9781637747711 (electronic)

Editing by Lydia Choi
Copyediting by Michael Fedison
Proofreading by Martha Gallant and Marissa Wold Uhrina
Text design and composition by Aaron Edmiston
Interior images by Melanie Cloth, Creative Lead at Zilker Media
Cover design by Paul McCarthy
Printed by Lake Book Manufacturing

This book is dedicated to my steadfast rock, my family.

To my loving husband, Jordan, thank you for being a true partner in every sense of the word. To my son, Landry, bringing you into this world while writing this book has been the greatest joy of my life. My favorite role is being your mom. To my parents, Mark and Cristina; Granna and Grandpa; my brother, Halen; and Doodle and Marsha, thank you for your unwavering support and the many sacrifices you made to give me every opportunity in life. But most of all, thank you for the unconditional love that has carried me every step of the way.

CONTENTS

Introduction

THE RISE OF THE STRATEGIC BUSINESS INFLUENCER

Sara Blakely was getting ready for a party when she realized she didn't have the right undergarment to provide a smooth look under white pants. Armed with scissors and sheer genius, she cut the feet off her control top pantyhose and the SPANX revolution began! With a focus on solving wardrobe woes, the SPANX brand has grown to offer bras, underwear, leggings, activewear, and more . . . Sara was named the world's youngest, self-made female billionaire by Forbes *magazine and one of* TIME's *100 Most Influential People.*[1]

Modern-day entrepreneur Sara Blakely started the billion-dollar company SPANX with a $0 marketing budget. She utilized her network, PR, social media, and customer word-of-mouth to educate her customers and make them feel like they were rooting for her personally, not merely buying the products of a faceless company. Many fans can quote details of her story displayed on her website from memory because she shared it consistently with conviction whenever she had an opportunity. This resulted in raving fans who could share how Sara started her company with just $5,000, how her first headquarters was in a spare bedroom, and how she carried her lucky red backpack everywhere, including when she closed her first big deal with Neiman Marcus. That backpack is now preserved on the wall of SPANX headquarters, and it's the icon of Sara's Red Backpack Fund, which elevates other female entrepreneurs.

The brand would never have gotten so big, so fast, without Sara's willingness to go store-to-store to educate consumers on the product, build valuable relationships with those who believed in her product, and share her personal vision and human vulnerability. There is no big SPANX corporate marketing campaign that skyrocketed the brand to a billion-dollar company. Sara took a grassroots approach, listening to her customers and bringing authentic visibility to her journey while growing SPANX through the press, speaking engagements, and social media channels. What was unique about Sara, and why many customers related to her, is that she never tried to be someone she was not. She knew she was different from the other leaders in the undergarments industry because she had a mission bigger than herself for women. Sara recalls in a video on her Instagram being the only woman in a meeting on the manufacturing floor, realizing she did not have the most money (only $5,000) or the most experience in the room, but knowing she probably cared the most. So she said:

> ## "LET ME SEE WHAT CAN HAPPEN IF I CARE THE MOST."

She leaned into that authenticity, making it her competitive advantage, even though she caught flack for it at the beginning of her career.

She often publicly shares most about her biggest failures and mishaps both in building SPANX and as a working mom, bringing a memorable sense of humor and self-deprecation relatable to any woman in her target audience.

Her bond with her fans is so intense that even when she decided to sell a majority stake in the company in October 2021, unlike nearly every other merger & acquisition announcement, which typically funnel through high-dollar PR firms and official press releases, she made the announcement via her personal Instagram account. Sara has since continued to use her platform to rally her audience around the SPANX brand and, more importantly, start new ventures that could serve her mission to advocate for women through products. In 2024, Sara launched her new venture, Sneex, a luxury hybrid high-heel sneaker. This new invention has not been welcomed with open arms in the fashion scene, but whether you like the product or not, the buzz around her launch was very different from the initial launch of her first product, SPANX. On her Instagram account, she shared how differently the marketing strategy of Sneex was compared to SPANX because she already had independently built an audience she could share her latest innovation with outside of SPANX corporate channel followers. Yes, Sara is now a billionaire, but she started like most entrepreneurs of small businesses, with measly funds in a personal bank account—but with one key difference: She saw the potential impact she could have by becoming a Strategic Business Influencer.

Strategic Business Influencer

noun

A business leader who develops high-touch, strong personalized connections, yet scalable relationships to accelerate trust and drive significant impact on their revenue and profits.

When you hear the word "influencer," who pops into your mind first? A teenager doing a makeup tutorial on YouTube? Soccer superstar Cristiano Ronaldo, with his 603 million Instagram followers? Kim Kardashian? Taylor Swift?

In the age of social media, such influencers have become a prominent force in shaping pop culture and consumer trends. They challenge norms, shift public opinion, and change what the rest of us are talking about, watching, and buying. But to ease your mind, mainstream or celebrity influencers are *not* what this book is about. The key to business success is not achieved by wacky stunts, dances, political rants, or celebrity gossip to rack up followers on TikTok or Instagram. I'm not encouraging you to record yourself all day and become a social media influencer—at least not how most people use that term. My focus for this book, rather, is on a class of leaders I call Strategic Business Influencers. They're usually not as famous as Ronaldo, Swift, or Kardashian, but they can be powerful role models for any executive or entrepreneur who wants to build a big brand with a small budget.

According to the US Small Business Administration, 99.9% of businesses in America are categorized as small businesses.[2] Even though the competition for small businesses is high, the reality is that budgets are low. It is up to leaders to build and execute a strategy that will rise above the noise and beat out the bigger competition with larger budgets on a consistent basis. Leaders who are visible in an authentic, mission-driven way give companies a competitive advantage that cannot be replicated: their leadership influence. Over the past decade, we have seen leaders carry more influence in the business world than corporate brands. This book will help you explore how to identify your influence and leverage it, not for fame, but to drive business results.

Strategic Business Influencers develop high-touch yet scalable relationships with their customers and other stakeholders by strategically leveraging intentional branding, social media, data acquisition, press, and related platforms. They build trust, credibility, and differentiation at a level previously reserved for big-company CEOs with big budgets. They use the intangible benefits of influence and accessible platforms to accelerate trust and drive a significant impact on their revenue and profits.

I believe the concept of business influencers actually began long before Sara and the internet, with the rise of famous entrepreneurs in the late 19th and early 20th centuries. Henry Ford built his personal brand in parallel with his company's brand. He is still known as one of the most memorable inventors, and his manufacturing business model, now called Fordism, has been used as inspiration for many other successful companies since then, including Google and Apple. Estée Lauder did the same while growing her beauty products empire after World War II. She was a leader known for being the Trojan horse of her product marketing, spearheading primarily word-of-mouth campaigns. She believed she would be the most trusted on-ramp for her customers back to her company and products. Her representation of the brand encouraged women to quickly spread the word about her products. Steve Jobs also established his footprint in the 1980s, when he made his personal coolness inseparable from that of the fledgling Apple Computer. Such leaders integrated their own personalities and expertise into their marketing strategies and word-of-mouth campaigns. They intentionally blurred the lines between a personal brand and a business brand. If you admired the face of a company, you were far more inclined to buy whatever it was selling.

Until the past decade or two, such superstar business influencers were as rare as the size of the businesses they built. Few leaders had the opportunity or resources to emulate Ford, Lauder, Jobs, Walt Disney, or Lee Iacocca. However, in the current environment, opportunities to become a Strategic Business Influencer extend to just about everyone—and just about every leader should recognize and seize those opportunities.

Growing up, I was a musician, singer, and songwriter. I had a unique upbringing going to school during the week and on weekends traveling across the country to play venues like the House of Blues, filming reality TV shows, being featured in national publications such as *CosmoGirl* (a Y2K publication—remember that one?) and *Texas Monthly*, and participating as talent for Radio Disney tours. I almost found myself in a full *Hannah Montana* scene. To be seen by talent agencies and bigwig record executives, you had to hit the pavement touring, which is challenging when balancing "a normal life" is just as important to your family. (A decision by my parents that served me well later in life, as I was only a preteen at the time.) Sure, I had a modest group of fans who traveled to shows, but it would take years to garner the listenership for the music I strived for without a record label to record and release my songs for mass consumption. See, back then, music was not accessible on the internet like it is today. There was no SoundCloud, YouTube, Spotify, or TikTok. I did get interest from managers, publishers, and record labels, but each came with a level of control over my image and music that was not worth the reward for me personally. I did not want anyone to dictate the color of my hair, what I wore, what message I conveyed in my songs, and the style of music I performed. Sound familiar? Many entrepreneurs begin their journey with this mindset around what they experience in their industry.

Now, as you might have guessed based on the biography found on the back of this book, I never hit the *Billboard* charts, and I veered away from building my career as a musician. But I did pick it back up in my twenties while living in Austin, Texas, known as the live music capital of the world, as a creative outlet and hobby. At that point, I was not into it for the fame. However, I was amazed at how different the landscape looked for musicians and how quickly traction could be generated with access to online platforms that did not exist in my preteen years. After filming a few poorly lit, low-audio-quality videos on my living room couch, I was booking paid weekly bar gigs, and in a matter of months, I had podcast interviews and was approached by a sponsor to upgrade my sound equipment. It became quite the little side hustle to bring in a small amount of disposable income and a fun way to get a free bar tab on the weekends. This new landscape excited me for young musicians because they now had accessibility and all of the control.

This development paved the way for musicians like Zach Bryan, who built a raving fan base and topped music charts before catching the attention of Nashville record labels. Zach is one of the first modern-day musicians who completely circumvented the need for traditional representation by leveraging direct access to his fan base. He enlisted in the Navy to follow in his veteran parents' footsteps at the age of seventeen and completed tours in Djibouti and Bahrain. Throughout his time in the Navy, Zach started writing songs in his free time and posting them on YouTube. After uploading sixteen songs, Zach found viral video success with his breakout song, "Heading South." After writing the song minutes earlier, he filmed the video on a phone outside of his Navy barracks in humid 95-degree heat. That video now has more than 30 million views several short years later. He later garnered more fame through TikTok, all while continuing his US Navy service and recording his first album with the help of his fellow servicemen at an Airbnb in Florida. Zach continued to grow his fan base by releasing songs online as he wrote them and made his Grand Ole Opry debut while still actively serving in the US military. It was not until late 2021 that he received an honorable discharge from the Navy to pursue his music career. Once established, Zach inked a deal for his own imprint under Warner Records, where he continues to write and produce his own music—and even signs his own artists. This approach has allowed him to continue fully calling the shots in his career. He has continued to utilize platforms to go against industry norms by partnering with AXS to prevent for-profit resale of concert tickets, keeping tickets reasonably priced for fans, and preventing secondary market inflation. Zach has also rejected the traditional album rollout model by releasing tracks frequently, sometimes without much promotion. He has been known to release more songs in one year than traditional artists release over multiple years. Through this strategy, Zach has now sold over a million albums and over 10 million singles since 2019.[3] Although he did not represent a company, Zach used tactics I will explore in this book, and that the music industry had never seen, to create a dominant yet authentic brand.

This book is about how to venture down the road of becoming a Strategic Business Influencer, even for leaders who think they or their businesses aren't interesting enough to qualify them as such. Let's consider an example in a space that's much less glamorous than undergarments and selling out stadiums—regional banking. Local entrepreneur Jeff Wilkinson founded Keystone Bank in Austin in 2018, aiming to develop high-touch relationships with the city's booming community of entrepreneurs. Keystone offered a consultative approach for entrepreneurs Jeff believed would set them apart from competing banks.

Jeff led his team to differentiate the regional banking experience for entrepreneurs in every way possible—from the look and feel of the brand using a crisp, high-end visual design normally only reserved for global banks, to investing in the technology that allowed business owners the mobile agility most needed but that they could not find outside of name-brand banks to help them accelerate their relationship-building and lead-generation strategy. His vision for Keystone blended an innovative regional bank experience with keeping the most important advantage of banking locally for an entrepreneur, which is the relationship. For any business owner, the most important asset of a local bank is the accessibility and relationship with decision-makers because they can give you the keys you need to open doors and see your vision come to life.

Jeff, a self-made entrepreneur, knew building and maximizing relationships with leaders in Austin's entrepreneurial community would be one of the most integral aspects of their strategy to master. Of course, he and his leadership team took the typical hands-on approach with coffees, lunches, and events, but this strategy was no different from how bankers in town traditionally built relationships. Jeff added a never-before-seen element to Keystone's relationship-building strategy that made their bank stand out to prospects and build a more meaningful connection.

As the Keystone team built their new downtown office, they displayed their sleek branding and created a high-end environment with beautiful interior design, but they also differentiated the in-office experience by setting up a podcast studio next to their conference rooms at the front of the bank. The podcast room proudly displayed a prominent "Keystone On Air" sign visible to the bustling street traffic. This piqued the curiosity of many customers who came into the bank. Jeff called the podcast *Banking on Community*, and the Keystone team used it as a reason to reach out to and invite Austin business leaders to be guests. When they came in to record their episode, his interviewees not only got a tour of the branch but also had an opportunity to sit down with the bank's chairman and CEO and talk about their leadership and business for over 45 minutes. Jeff's podcast became a platform for meaningful discussions, shedding light on industry insights, market trends, and useful takeaways for listeners.

Before long, Keystone had a unique brand image as a friend to the Austin entrepreneurial community. It redefined the traditional banking experience, giving its customers a unique platform for dialogue and connection. As Jeff's strategy business influencer approach paid off, Keystone became the fastest-growing regional bank in Texas. Jeff has also since been named one of the best CEOs in Austin and landed a spot on *Austin Business Journal*'s coveted Austin Power Players list, next to names like Matthew McConaughey and Kendra Scott.

From regional banking to subfloor manufacturing, women's undergarments to tech software development, becoming a Strategic Business

Influencer builds undeniable leverage for a brand, no matter the industry or business size. I'm passionate about sharing this strategy because I believe everyday entrepreneurs can change the world for the better—I've seen it repeatedly. I've encountered too many leaders not reaching their full impact and stunting their growth because they have stayed fully behind the scenes. As the cofounder and CEO of Zilker Media, I've made it my life's work to help entrepreneurs worldwide become Strategic Business Influencers.

I first got into this mission by a mixture of a little bit of happenstance, good luck, and hard work that turned into a life passion. I started my career off by exploring work in entertainment PR, retail marketing, and digital strategy for political campaigns. What stuck and ignited my passion for working with business leaders was when I landed a job at a non-fiction book PR and marketing agency in Austin, Texas, called Shelton Interactive. This is where I first cut my teeth in working with the world's leading CEOs, founders, and executives to establish their brands ahead of their book launches. At Shelton Interactive we worked on over 30 *New York Times* and *Wall Street Journal* bestselling business books. Several years later, after launching some of the top business books in the genre, we had an exciting agency strategic acquisition and, not long after, the opportunity to start a new agency alongside my business partner Rusty Shelton, the founder of Shelton Interactive, and a few other key founding team members. When we sat down in 2017 to build out the mission and vision of Zilker Media, we made the decision to broaden the application of what we did so well with authors for PR, strategic content creation, and branding in the previous agency to corporate leaders and the companies they lead—and we haven't looked back since.

What I've seen over the past decade in my work is that the environment for leaders has changed, and an invisible, behind-the-scenes-only leadership style no longer serves you or your company. In fact, this dated approach to leadership can now cause more harm than good. I aim to help leaders with grit, vision, and passion step into a modern CEO role to build a scalable impact and stand out against their larger competitors. I'm passionate about this because I want to see leaders succeed—especially leaders of small to medium-sized businesses struggling to compete with much bigger competitors. Leading your marketing with a logo-versus-logo strategy will never beat out your larger rivals. If leaders do not shift their approach, they will be left behind. My mission is to ensure small to medium-sized businesses stay thriving and even come out on top.

If you feel like you are too early in your business, or even if you feel like you are too late in your career, the strategy in this book also applies directly to you. You might already be apprehensive about this approach because you fear coming across as egotistical or overly self-promotional. Counterintuitively, I'd argue that kind of initial gut reaction is a good sign. In fact, you are precisely the kind of leader I wrote this book for! As you'll read in the pages to come, becoming a Strategic Business Influencer is not an exercise in becoming a personality or celebrity; it's an unbeatable way to convey your expertise, trustworthiness, and credibility to customers, investors, and employees in a way that serves them, your team, and your partners along the way.

Megan Gluth, owner and CEO of Catalynt, the largest women-owned supplier of raw materials in North America, initially viewed building her brand as "self-promoting and self-aggrandizing." Megan shared that she initially had to overcome a few mental hurdles but realized what she had to offer could help others in a way that would ultimately fulfill her.

When my team and I first discussed building my brand, I thought, God, the last thing I need is another thing to do. *And I don't think I'm alone in thinking like that. When you're an executive, you can look at your brand as just another dreaded to-do item on your list, but I've been surprised at how easy it has been to put energy into building my brand because it authentically reflects me in every way. What you see online is really what you get. Staying true to this is important because people will google you before they sit down with you. When what they see matches who I am when I walk into a room, my brand becomes more credible. When doing a business deal such as an acquisition, you have a team of lawyers, investment bankers, and all those fancy people in a room. But at the end of the day, the deal comes down to trust alone. You've got to trust me, and I've got to trust you. Everything goes away if there is no trust. You cannot build trust without an authentic brand. The interesting thing I've encountered since making my story more visible is I see people coming to meetings with a little bit more of their humanity, which I just think makes better business. If I have something to say that could help even one person, that would be fulfilling for me.*[4]

Do you have a similar gut reaction to building your brand as Megan did? Most leaders I meet with do because they share Megan's mindset when it comes to impact. At the end of the day, it is not only your success but also how fulfilled you are in that success that matters. Your goal shouldn't be gaining millions of followers; it should be connecting with the *right* 500 followers who can make a huge difference to the success of your business and career.

Throughout this book, I will share the stories of leaders from a wide range of fields, from business moguls to gritty small business entrepreneurs, who have successfully built big brands with small budgets. I will also share a framework you can run with to execute this powerful strategy and create results for your business without having to quit your day job along the way. First, we will look at the six steps required to become a Strategic Business Influencer.

SIX STEPS TO INFLUENCE

Whitney Wolfe Herd was deeply shaken by the emotional turbulence she endured.

She was cofounder of Tinder and its VP of Marketing until she resigned in 2014 under a cloud of intense controversy and a lawsuit alleging sexual harassment. While under fire in proceedings, Whitney faced public humiliation and online harassment for months through the media and social media platforms. Although she understandably recounts this as a dark time in her life, Whitney turned to her experiences to create a brand that would combat the problem she and so many others experienced: dangerous online spaces. She was determined to make a change.

She channeled resilience to move past the public scrutiny and built a brand that empowered women everywhere by flipping the dating process on its head. Within months of leaving Tinder, she launched Bumble as a female-driven alternative to other dating apps on the market. Like other dating apps at the time, Bumble users could swipe right if they liked a dating profile and/or swipe left if they didn't to sort through and match with potential partners. But Bumble's unique feature was if a man and a woman both swiped right and matched, only the woman could reach out and send the first message. This unique feature empowered women to make the first move and allowed for a safer online dating environment because women were no longer inundated with unwanted, toxic messages many receive on other dating apps. On Bumble, women were fully in control of the communication they could receive.

To provide full transparency, I'm not a paid promoter for Bumble. But I'm grateful Whitney dared to launch Bumble in December 2014 because that is how I met my husband in my early twenties. That's right . . . I swiped right!

Over the next few years, Whitney brilliantly kept brand versus tech at Bumble's core—a rarity in the tech world that kept Bumble at the forefront of the online dating market and true to its mission. It was the first company in the tech scene to implement behavioral and content moderation as part of its business model, banning well over 880,000 users from the platform over the years.

Whitney launched Bumble with a grassroots-style marketing campaign before the app was even available. In an interview with CNBC, she described the early days of her efforts by saying, "We did not have countless marketing dollars . . . we actually had to be really scrappy."[5] Due to her modest start-up budget, she traveled every weekend to integrate the brand into college campus sororities and fraternities, sharing its mission and, most importantly, her "why." She used nontraditional tactics to create experiences around the brand that made users talk about Bumble in their networks, ultimately creating a viral effect that snowballed over time. Through hosting branded sorority panty parties and fraternity Bumble-branded pizza parties and utilizing these experiences to educate on the brand's mission, demand was born across campuses to be part of the online community.

While building demand for the brand, Whitney faced many rejections from investors who doubted that the concept would ever be adopted because it went against societal norms. Instead of taking this feedback as a need to change her approach, mission, or how she presented herself, she used this rejection to fuel her belief in herself. Whitney leaned into this doubt and shared her personal experiences in a real, public way that actually accelerated her company. As her company grew, she seemed to bring more visibility to her raw authenticity as a leader.

Rapid growth enabled Bumble to go public in February 2021, when Whitney was only 31, making her the youngest female CEO to ever take a company public. The moment she became a self-made billionaire and took the company public, she strategically used the time the cameras were on her to further her brand's impact. She remotely approached the NASDAQ bell at her headquarters in Austin, called the Beehive, turned around, grabbed her one-year-old son from her husband, and rang the opening bell with him on her hip. This was, of course, a move that went viral, shifting the anticipated media headlines and social media captions to a controlled, memorable narrative reinforcing her mission versus the typical—and, most of the time, forgettable—CEO profile and business stats. Every headline that day mentioned her action at that moment. And within a few hours of the IPO, Bumble's stock was up 63%.

Even as a tech titan, Whitney shared in many interviews that she often faced impostor syndrome throughout her entrepreneurial journey. Being a Strategic Business Influencer didn't come naturally to her, but she recognized the importance of creating a direct relationship with her audience and committed to it.

Statistics show she's not alone in that initial apprehension. Global consulting firm Korn Ferry reported in its 2024 Workforce Global Insights report that 71% of US CEOs experience impostor syndrome in their role.[6] Many leaders hesitate to make the visible step out from behind their business because they face this challenge. You might be telling yourself that you do not feel qualified enough to become a Strategic Business

Influencer. I believe you are wrong, just like Whitney Wolfe Herd was wrong, and I will share stories from many other CEOs throughout this book who also had to overcome this limiting belief. My goal is to help you uncover the areas where you are already driving influence and value with clients, partners, investors, and employees and show you how to amplify them at scale to generate tangible results for your business.

Indeed, the top hiring and matching platform in the world, defines the eight key responsibilities of a CEO in the following order:[7]

- Representing the company
- Strategic planning
- Overseeing strategic implementation
- Executive evaluation
- Monitoring markets
- Risk minimization
- Setting corporate policy
- Communicating with a board of directors

Research and insights from *Forbes*,[8] Trainual,[9] and *Harvard Business Review*[10] all affirm these themes as crucial responsibilities for the top leader in a business. Of course, how granular these activities are depends on the size of your business. I believe to achieve success as a CEO, your time should be spent narrowing in on the above eight categories. As you analyze this list and where you spend your time, you might find that no matter the business or the environment, these responsibilities hold true. The approach to leaning into these responsibilities and driving results for your business has evolved over time. If you were to approach some of these responsibilities even the way you did a few years ago, the results would not be nearly as effective in today's environment. That is because the goalpost has changed for many CEOs in what influences success in business. Research shows CEOs in today's landscape will be judged not only by their financial success but also by the influential impact they have on employees, customers, and their communities. Because of this, analysis from the National Institute of Standards and Technology shows that trust is the most vital asset a CEO needs to build because it alone will accelerate a leader's ability to create a competitive advantage.[11]

In reality, the ability to master these responsibilities today requires a different mindset for leaders. The modern-day CEO still needs to build a competitive differentiation for their business and trust among their stakeholders, but the road map to accomplishing that now looks completely different. The leaders who are willing to step out from behind the scenes to build influence alongside their business with the *right* audiences will dominate over those who continue leading with a faceless corporate logo because they have a leg up on the speed with which they can gain influence and trust with their audiences.

Your audience is no longer looking to connect with the most polished brand content, sleek advertisements, or activations—they are looking to connect with everyday people who are authentic, passionate, entertaining storytellers and educators. Edelman's 2024 Trust Barometer Global Report found that 74% of respondents now trust peers who they see more like themselves just as much as they trust traditional figures of authority such as scientists, physicians, or public office holders.[12] No matter the industry, this shift is imperative. The *Wall Street Journal* covered this phenomenon even rippling among American blue-collar workers, citing a movement of plumbers and construction workers bringing visibility to the work they do daily in an effort to make blue-collar work "cool again."[13] As blue-collar influencers grew, enrollment in vocational schools among the younger generation did as well. Blue-collar influencers have been shown to inspire thousands of young Americans to enter trade work to seek out careers that avoid student debt and desks and that have autonomy.

Authentic influencers are the new trust factor in today's business environment and, as such, Strategic Business Influencers at the helm of companies can now hold more power than the media, paid advertising, or any corporate brand. So, what does it take to make this shift as a leader? If you are reading this in a panic, you most likely have two thoughts coming to mind.

1. Where in the world am I going to find time for this? I already have too many more important things on my plate.
2. What if promoting my personal brand comes off as self-serving? I, in no way, want my company to be about me.

Thoughts like this also first came to the minds of everyday Strategic Business Influencers Jack Aspenson and Joyce Durst. The CEO of a multimillion-dollar subflooring manufacturer, Jack Aspenson shared what drives him as a Strategic Business Influencer. He wants his ventures to be known to "create secure and safe communities. Everything I do is about creating communities. When people ask what I do, I oftentimes tell them I fix problems. That normally elicits great follow-up conversation." In our discussion, Jack went on to share that he didn't become an entrepreneur for fame or money. He knows there is often more risk entrepreneurs face when it comes to money. Jack shared this about what he hopes to influence as a leader:

> *You run into people that are in it for themselves. I've never been in it for the money myself. Yes, I work to provide a comfortable living for my family, but I want to leave a legacy. Creating safe and secure communities and building a legacy have always been important to me. But I also look at my influence as a way to help other people grow and succeed in life. And hopefully, inspire some of them to start their own businesses.*[14]

EY Entrepreneur of the Year Gulf South award winner Joyce Durst had similar sentiments that propelled her past the two barriers I mentioned above, sharing, "This journey cannot just be about money. If it is, there are many easier ways to make money—go work for a big company. But if you really wanna do something good for the world, if you really wanna do something good for people, you have got to find your why and let that be your driver every single day." Joyce went on to share the transformational impact her business has seen once she took the steps to become a Strategic Business Influencer:

> *The impact the visibility has had on our company cannot be overstated. It's so funny, because I'm an introvert by nature. It is strange for me when I go places now, and people will say, "Oh, I know you! Your company has won all these awards." This type of visibility has brought us things I could have never had an equivalent amount of marketing dollars to afford. There's no way we would have ever had that kind of money to garner that exposure traditionally.*[15]

In the following chapters, we will explore how Jack and Joyce built their companies as Strategic Business Influencers. But I tell their stories to assure you that this book is not about building a self-serving personal brand or adding more to your plate as a leader. My goal is to protect your time by focusing on the mission-driven activities you are already doing daily that are high value for you. This book will teach you to bring visibility to the right audience to make a greater impact on your responsibilities as a leader.

Most people who attempt to build their brand this way jump right into building visibility with outward tactics such as public relations, social media, advertising campaigns, or email marketing. As entrepreneurs, we cannot stifle our innate need to go straight to action. However, building a winning impact as a Strategic Business Influencer requires intentionality in getting your brand foundation right. Just like building your business, you have to do the groundwork first to build lasting infrastructure.

Throughout this book, we will explore a six-step framework to build your brand as a Strategic Business Influencer. As a modern CEO, I want to prevent you from falling into traditional marketing traps tailored only for big budgets. We will first look at three steps that will require some front-end work but are necessary for today's leaders. This strategy work will keep your brand grounded with an inward focus to:

1. Create your "Influence ID."
2. Evaluate your first impression.
3. Build a foundation for audience ownership.

Once the groundwork is complete, the next three steps use that inward preparation to win over customers, investors, partners, and employees:

4. Create PR buzz from your smartphone.
5. Develop content that drives leads.
6. Turbocharge your referrals.

After we go through each step, I will show how to combine them into a unified, powerful strategy that drives results for your business. I will focus on the areas best served by your time, ensuring you do not quit your day job to build success with this strategy.

Throughout these six steps, I will share examples of inspiring companies and leaders from various sizes and fields, including quite a few that my company has worked with personally, to unpack how this strategy can be applied no matter your industry or subject matter expertise. I want to shift your strategy—and mindset—to drive visibility for your mission, business, and personal passions with the activities you are already doing as a leader every day.

Positioning yourself as a Strategic Business Influencer brings you to the crossroads of personal fulfillment, business growth, and significant impact. You may not realize this, but building your brand as a Strategic Business Influencer will become one of your favorite activities as a CEO because it centers around the impact you can make on others every day. This will lead you to achieve success—whatever that looks like for you—while rivaling industry giants. The question I want you to ask yourself as we get started is simple.

Where are you missing opportunities to drive value for your . . .

. . . business?

. . . employees?

. . . partners?

. . . investors?

. . . family?

. . . friends?

By the end of this book, you will be able to answer these questions, and I'm confident the steps we will walk through will serve as a catalyst for the meaningful impact you can make as a leader. Let's dive in on how to build a big brand with a small budget.

PART 1

Step 1

CREATE YOUR "INFLUENCE ID"

Who are you *in addition* to being an entrepreneur?

I first asked this question in 2019 while facilitating a retreat workshop in a room of 12 entrepreneurs with businesses grossing over $50 million in revenue annually. The once rambunctious, lively room discussing marketing strategies fell completely silent when that question was asked. So much so you could hear the spa music drifting down the hall of the upscale resort. I did not anticipate the blank stares I would receive at that moment, and they did not anticipate I would ask them to describe themselves beyond the business—after all, this was a business retreat.

While some of the leaders in the room were preparing to take their businesses to the next level, others were preparing for an exit in the next five years. As we went person by person around the U-shaped room, some answered the question by listing characteristics such as parent, friend, and advocate, while others point-blank said they "needed more time to think." With their goals in mind, I knew each leader would be walking into future rooms to represent their companies against their competitors to attract multi-year contracts, investors, and even buyers. Their visibility and preparation for their next chapter as leaders would be crucial. Based on the hesitant response, we threw out the agenda for the remainder of the day and spent the rest of our time workshopping this question for each leader. The moment after I walked out of that room, I knew it was mission-critical to help entrepreneurs define their brands as Strategic Business Influencers.

So, how about you?

Who are you *in addition* to being an entrepreneur?

It is a simple yet challenging question. Just like that room of entrepreneurs, you might feel a little hesitant trying to come up with an answer. As leaders, we obsessively spend our time around the clock thinking about how we can improve our companies. Our identities as leaders can sometimes be so heads down in our business that we discount why loyal customers were attracted to working with us, investors believed in us, or employees got behind the mission in the first place. Your customers, investors, and employees did not choose to work with you because of your meticulously crafted 12-page business plan. Honestly, most probably will not take the time to read through that plan page by page. The reason why they choose to work with your business and support its growth is, most likely, you. They believed in your vision, leadership, and ability to execute. Most importantly . . . they *trusted* you.

YOU ARE MORE THAN YOUR BUSINESS

When at conferences or networking events, how often are you asked, "What do you do?" or prompted, "Why don't you tell me a little bit about yourself?"

How do you answer these questions?

Do you naturally blurt out your job title or your company's

well-crafted elevator pitch? These are not bad responses; they are just as commoditized as it gets—the same as everyone else. So how do you stand out from every other leader in the room? The answer is not by improving your company's elevator pitch. Simply put, you stand out by conveying more of yourself in an authentic and visible way.

Many leaders get stumped when thinking through who they are because they want to avoid being pigeonholed into one subject area or feel like they cannot visibly display different aspects of their lives because they might "not fit" into the current business agenda. The uniqueness of a Strategic Business Influencer versus a corporate logo is there are many facets that make up your brand that you bring influence to. If you think about the way you have approached building professional relationships over the years, when you sit down in a room with another person, it is not a robotic sales pitch that wins. It has been proven that the most successful engagements start with the ability to connect with someone on a human level.[1] It might be a commonality of an upbringing, favorite sports team, children around the same age, vision, or philanthropic involvement that solidifies a connection with the other person. Of course, success cannot be built on those commonalities alone, but they begin to build a foundation of trust. As a Strategic Business Influencer, you need to have the ability to both create a connection and deliver a quality product or service, but effective leaders in today's environment must be able to build trust and create a connection at scale. Put simply, if you reserve the ability to discover connection points and subject matter expertise for one-on-one, in-person meetings, you limit your ability to scale your impact as a leader to the number of hours you have in a day.

To get past the fallacy that you have to present yourself to fit in a mold, I want you to visualize your brand as a wheel.

Your brand as a Strategic Business Influencer serves as the hub of this wheel. Each individual spoke coming from the hub is an area your brand represents. You might have spokes of your wheel representing different

Your Brand Wheel

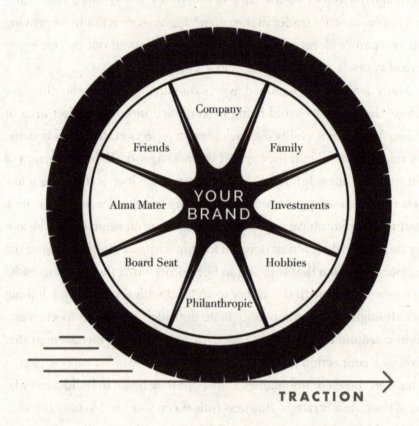

ventures such as your alma mater, hobbies, family, philanthropic causes, board seats, or religion. These spokes all connect your hub to the rest of the wheel to allow for traction and movement. Just like people, there are different models of wheels that have a different number of spokes that derive from the hub. As an entrepreneur, it is in your DNA to be the connection point to multiple spokes. So why put barriers on your visibility that limit the areas you can create impact for? Strategic Business Influencers are meant to be multidimensional—we are people. Our brands should reflect that depth and not be confined to a single, limiting narrative.

Once you have identified all of the spokes you represent in your life, the next step is to craft a strategy to convey your impact. This strategy should not only bring visibility to your different spokes but also communicate your broader influence. Think of it as a way to genuinely articulate your value, authenticity, and differentiation to your audience. In the rest of this chapter, I will guide you through a process I call developing your Influence ID to help you do just that.

ISSUING YOUR INFLUENCE ID

The Influence ID framework is the foundation of your brand positioning, helping to identify how you want to be perceived, the influence you currently have, and the impact you want to make moving forward. The ID card you create becomes the connection point for all aspects of your personal and professional life to tell your story in a way that resonates with others and drives connection and trust. It sounds elementary, but I promise you if you do not have the right framework, it can tend to feel more complex than you think. This is why we only see a select number of leaders master their ID while others tend to get stuck. Often, business leaders tell me the process is more taxing than creating their corporate brand identity because it requires both an introspective and intraspective thought process. Unfortunately, creating your Influence ID is a step you cannot miss. If you jump to the second half of this book straight to the fun of PR and content marketing, without your ID, you will hinder the success you can achieve as a Strategic Business Influencer and have less fun and impact. This is why I've worked to distill the creation of your Influence ID into a simple-to-follow process.

I liken creating your Influence ID to filling out a passport application. When you first apply for a passport, you are filling out an application to ultimately obtain access to places you have not been before. To get there, you must first fill out the application with information about where you came from, such as your date of birth, where you were born, who your parents were, your marital status, and other names you may have used in the past. You will also be asked to include up-to-date information, such as your social security number, current name, physical address, occupation, phone number, height, and hair and eye color. There is even a portion of your application where you must list your upcoming travel plans, including desired destinations and dates. Once you fill out all of the information, you will also be asked to submit supplemental documents such as a current picture and birth certificate to affirm credibility that you are who you say you are. After the application is reviewed and approved, the final product will represent where you came from, where you are now, and where you want to go, all in a matter of one page. Your passport book will provide you with pages to add travel stamps to keep an updated profile of your journeys for years to come.

As you know, with filling out a passport application, the end result of having access to travel internationally is rewarding, but it takes a little work on the front end to gather all the information and get you there. This is why I have created a simple, five-step process that will lead you to create your Influence ID. Think of this framework as your expedited passport service.

Step 1: Where You Came From and Where You Want to Go

I was standing onstage speaking for the first time with over 150 of the nation's top physicians and healthcare professionals in the crowd nodding their heads, applauding, shooting their hands up to ask questions, and rushing toward me to dive deeper into their brand at the end of a three-hour-long thought leadership marketing workshop at a Harvard Medical School conference. That moment in Boston's historic Fairmont Copley Plaza ballroom was the first time I realized teaching leaders at scale was a fulfilling passion for me. It was not fulfilling because I wanted to be center stage. It was quite the opposite, actually.

I'll let you in on a secret only those who know me best understand. I'm severely introverted in a crowded room, so the idea of getting on a stage and speaking to a crowd that size gave me crippling anxiety. The stage was really the last place I wanted to be standing in a room that big. I had spent years consulting and teaching one-on-one and with teams, but speaking in front of a crowd this size was another story. I remember thinking to myself the night before, *If only I could sing for three hours tomorrow about branding—that would feel more natural to me.* I grew up singing onstage, which felt second nature to me, but I hardly ever had to speak in front of crowds. I quickly ditched the singing fantasy because I knew this crowd did not sign up for a bad version of *High School Musical.* While preparing for the workshop, I also had to battle the head trash of impostor syndrome. I found I was repeatedly asking myself, *What in the world do I have to teach these doctors who are actually curing cancer?*

Have you ever questioned the value of what you can share with others?

I was clammy walking onstage after being introduced, but all of these thoughts and feelings vanished as I started talking with the crowd. The feeling of fulfillment I get when working with clients one-on-one was multiplied, and I was able to experience what it was like to create an impact at a scale beyond the clients I have had the opportunity to work with daily. This feeling was similar to what I had experienced in my past as a musician watching guitar riffs and melodic lyrics move people from a stage. Weeks and months after speaking at that conference, I heard from physicians who experienced thought leadership success in their fields and significant growth in their impact. It was incredibly meaningful to be able to help a crowd of over 150 and watch a true ripple effect. My apprehension about speaking changed after that conference because my mindset shifted from worry about the attention being on me to the impact opportunity I was neglecting if I did not speak more. Because of this experience, the next year, I decided to set goals for teaching and speaking to groups alongside my usual annual business goals. While setting these goals, I knew one of the greatest stages to make a difference as a speaker would be a TEDx event. So I put TEDx on my five-year road map, knowing I would need additional experience and key activities to accomplish this goal. The road map to reaching that goal over the next five years included homing in on the right topic, gathering speaking testimonies, increasing the frequency of talks, and continuing to get feedback on ways to improve my talk to result in maximum impact. This goal-setting road map exercise completely shifted my mindset, trajectory, and where I focused my time over the next five years. At the end of year four, I received an email from a fellow Entrepreneur Organization (EO) Austin chapter member about a TEDx event that was being hosted by the University of Texas at Austin. I knew this was the opportunity I had been working toward, and completed my application and shared case studies, experience, testimonials, and speaking video footage that I had worked to accumulate as part of my goals over the past four years.

It was four years and eleven months to the date when I took the stage at the TEDx event. It was an honor to speak on one of the world's largest platforms for thought and impact, but alongside that, I saw accelerated growth for my business because I could get the message to leaders out faster than working only one-on-one. In that moment, I was able to reflect back on when I set that goal and the past five years of work it took to get to that platform.

I've found setting clear, specific goals requires deep reflection.[2] Sometimes, it can be challenging to pause and look around as you venture toward your goal. For entrepreneurs, the goalpost is always moving. It is important to pause, though, and reflect to uncover where you are and how you got there. Understanding your past empowers you to shape your future more effectively. Intentional, deep reflection also helps you convey potential connection points for your audience that can lead to influence and empathy. Ask yourself some of the following questions during your reflection.

- What have I accomplished so far?
- What am I most proud of?
- What are the challenges I have faced?
- What are the things that have brought me joy?
- How am I motivated?
- Am I spending my time wisely?
- Who has had the greatest impact on my life?
- What are the things that concern me the most?
- What do I want most in the future?
- What am I grateful for?

To help walk you through this five-step "Influence ID" process, let's consider an entrepreneur and a scenario I've created as an example—we'll call this entrepreneur Cameron H. Block. Here's the scenario: Cameron is the founder of Supply Focus Now, a business-to-business software platform streamlining supply chain operations for mid-sized manufacturing companies. He started his career as a supply chain analyst and grew frustrated with the inefficiencies and lack of user-friendly tools in the industry, so he decided to start and scale his own company. As he reflected on his past, he thought about his experiences working in a family-owned manufacturing business to becoming an expert in supply chain optimization. He recalled the "aha moment" of identifying how outdated processes created bottlenecks and his drive to build a solution to solve them. Now that he has established his business and is looking to scale it moving forward, he started to think about what it could mean to establish himself as a thought leader in supply chain innovation. Cameron workshopped and listed the following personal goals to pave the way for where he wants to go.

Long-term goals for the next five years:

- Expand his leadership internationally by participating in global supply chain panels and summits, building relationships that open doors for Supply Focus Now in international markets.

- Establish the "Focus Leadership Academy" and personally teach quarterly leadership workshops to inspire and retain top talent.

- Be recognized on industry lists like Forbes Next 1000, not to highlight his leadership but to position Supply Focus Now as a game changer in the B2B space.

Goals for the next three years:

- Launch a podcast called *Modern Supply* where he'll interview peers, partners, and thought leaders. This will double as a platform to build relationships and credibility in the industry.

- Create a "Women in Supply Chain" mentorship initiative, positioning the company as a champion for diversity in the industry while cultivating a pipeline of exceptional talent.

- Keynote industry conferences like CSCMP EDGE, sharing his journey and lessons learned, which will simultaneously elevate Supply Focus Now's visibility and attract leads and talent.

Focus over the next year:

- Increase lead generation by hosting roundtables with mid-sized manufacturers, inviting industry leaders to discuss supply chain challenges.

- Write an article for *IndustryWeek*, sharing practical insights to promote his personal mission to modernize supply chains.

- Guest lecture at his alma mater to garner more experience speaking and create a pipeline for young talent.

As you work toward your goals, I encourage you to apply similar tactics to set goals for your business—just widen your mindset to also include where you will be personally alongside each of those milestones. One of my favorite methodologies to follow when goal setting is Gino Wickman's Traction system.[3] He encourages leaders to drill down and prioritize three to seven goals over a five- to ten-year period. From there, he has you create a road map of incremental milestones to accomplish your ten-year vision by evaluating what needs to be achieved by five-year, three-year, one-year, and quarterly targets. This breakdown of your goals and measured approach increases your chances of success in achieving your ten-year vision. I've seen the goals of Strategic Business Influencers be all over the map. Some entrepreneurs are building their brands to launch their dream companies, attract future board roles, become bestselling authors, exit their companies to turn around and launch new ventures, or start a philanthropic foundation. The beauty is that your Influence ID can be created at any point in your entrepreneurial journey. It is never too late to set a new goal and apply for access to where you want to go.

Step 2: Identify Areas of Differentiation

It can be challenging to identify what makes you unique, but the good news is you do not need to uncover these findings on your own. Enlist the support of two to three close confidants to help you see these areas and uncover potential blind spots through a series of what I call ID strategy interviews. Select at least one person who has been a peer or colleague in your professional career and at least one who knows you outside of the boardroom. This is similar to a 360 feedback tool, only less intimidating. Below is a bank of questions to pull from during your ID strategy interviews. These questions can be discussed over a quick call, coffee meeting, or dinner.

- What three to five words would you use to describe me?
- What three to five words do you believe *do not* best describe me?
- What areas of life and/or business do you believe I can add value to?
- What sets me apart from others?
- What are my strengths?
- Where are my areas of opportunity?
- Do you have an example of how you have seen me impact someone else's business or life?
- Have I impacted you in any way?
- What do you value most about me?
- What could make me more effective as a leader/mother/spouse/friend?

Use the following follow-up statements and questions to dive deeper into each question above.

- Can you share more about why you answered this way?
- What other thoughts do you have?
- How have you seen me display this in the past?
- And what else?

At this stage in the process, your goal is to collect as much data as possible from the people in your life you value the most. These are the people that will know who you are at your core. Their answers might affirm your reflections in step 1, but more than likely, you will unearth insights that take you by surprise. These ID strategy interviews not only uncover who you are to others, but they also articulate who you are *not*. My hope is this exercise is encouraging and will build confidence in helping you see areas of differentiation that you have discounted for years because it has always been second nature.

After conducting all of your ID strategy interviews, spend time analyzing the data collected. What were the themes you heard over and over? List those out in one column on a sheet of paper. Pay close attention to what language and adjectives were used by others. You will want to reflect these in your ID.

Are there any additional themes you would add to that list from your time of self-reflection? Write those down, too, under your current list.

Let's return to our pretend entrepreneur, Cameron H. Block. Cameron interviewed two executives on his leadership team and his lifelong friend. He listed the following themes each confidant touched on. Some of these themes were reaffirming to Cameron, and some he was surprised by.

360 EXERCISE THEMES
Analytical
Forward thinking
Approachable
Trusted
Visionary problem-solver
Mentor
Collaborative innovator
Adaptable and resilient
Advocate

After he listed the key themes he gleaned from the conversations with his closest circle, he listed out in a new column the three long-term goals he set in step 1. Looking at these next to each other allowed him to quickly identify potential alignment between the columns.

360 EXERCISE THEMES	LONG-TERM GOALS
Analytical	Expand leadership internationally.
Forward thinking	Inspire and retain top talent with the "Leadership Focus Academy."
Approachable	Garner visibility as a game changer by being featured on industry lists like Forbes Next 1000.
Trusted	Build relationships and credibility in the industry through a podcast.
Visionary problem-solver	Keynote industry conferences like CSCMP EDGE.

Now, list out to the side of your themes in a new column the three to five goals you set in step 1. Review these two columns side by side. Are there any themes listed that could align with your goals?

Draw connection points to the characteristics and themes that you could leverage to help you achieve each goal. Understanding where these connection points are will be the basis for creating your Influence ID.

Through this exercise, Cameron realized that his advocacy and presence could be leveraged to expand his leadership visibility internationally if he brought more visibility to it in the right way. He also discovered that his team saw him as forward thinking and innovative in his industry, which gave him more confidence to leverage those characteristics to approach and build relationships with industry thought leaders he could include in his network of future podcast guests.

Step 3: Define Your Four Content Pillars

How do you keep track of your ID once you reach your destination? It can be easy to get caught up in all the areas where you could spend your time as a leader. But as in business, if you are trying to do too many things, most of the time, you accomplish almost nothing. As an entrepreneur, the stakes are too high for that to happen with your impact. To keep track of your ID, create four distinct content pillars to serve as guardrails toward your mission and goals. Start with a statement for each pillar, then give a two- to three-sentence description of what each statement means. To craft this, draw on the differentiation themes you established from your reflection and ID strategy interviews in step 2 to determine your top four content pillars. These pillars should reinforce areas where you have credentialed experience affirmed by others while shining light on aspirations of where you want to go. When crafting your pillars, keep authenticity at the forefront. Do not get caught up trying to make them sound sexy or flashy. Remember, you are not trying to sell anything. If you feel like your tendency is to lean that way, keep your content pillars grounded in authenticity by categorizing them into three areas: your business experience, your personal experience, and your mission and passion.

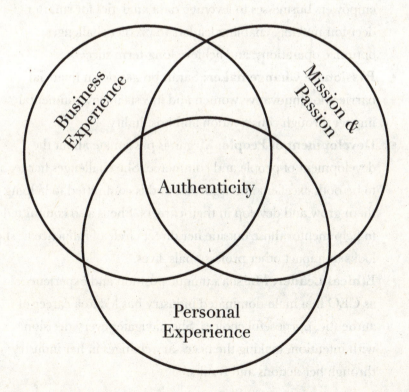

Balancing your content pillars in these circles will allow you to communicate your differentiation genuinely as a leader. The more descriptive your pillars are, the more clarity you have on the opportunities that align with your ID, which activities are worth your time, and what kind of impact you will make. Below are the content pillar descriptions from several Strategic Business Influencers from various industries.

- **Impactful Visionary:** With resolute determination and a clear road map in hand, David consistently brings his ideas to life, converting abstract concepts into practical outcomes with efficiency and precision. This focused approach empowers him to manifest his ideas, transforming them from vision to reality not only for himself, but also for his peers.

- **Champion of Data-Driven Decision-Making:** Jason empowers businesses to leverage data analytics for smarter decision-making, enabling leaders to predict challenges, optimize operations, and achieve long-term success.

- **Passionate Changemaker:** Sarah breaks down financial barriers for innovative women and invests in environmental impact through conservation and hospitality.

- **Development of People:** Megan is passionate about the development of people and commerce. She challenges her team to be both excellent and rigorous, and is committed to helping them grow and develop in their careers. She is also committed to help mentor those outside her direct circle of influence as she looks to impact other professionals' lives.

- **Ethical Leader:** Marsha's unique position and experience as CEO in a male-dominated industry has led to a career of authentic, purposeful choices. She navigates every decision with intention, making the necessary changes in her industry through her actions and results.

There is no right or wrong when it comes to your content pillars because, as you can see from the various examples above, they are a fully customized reflection of you. Use the insights from the ID strategy interviews to craft language that clearly articulates how you want to convey your influence to your audience. Your pillars are meant to be an internal compass while your brand and company grow to leverage for impact.

After aligning themes from the 360 to his goals in step 2, Cameron worked on crafting the following content pillars.

- **Practical Innovation:** Sharing user-friendly solutions and tools to modernize supply chains.
- **Future-Proofing Businesses:** Discussing strategies to stay agile amid global supply chain disruptions.
- **Data-Driven Decision-Making:** Teaching companies how to leverage analytics for efficiency and growth.
- **Empowering Mid-Sized Manufacturers:** Advocating for equitable access to tools traditionally reserved for enterprise-level companies.

These pillars will serve as a guideline of where he should focus his energy—whether speaking on panels, writing blog posts, or posting on LinkedIn.

If you find yourself getting writer's block crafting your pillars, one trick is to write these descriptions in the third person as these Strategic Business Influencers did. Sometimes, this perspective allows you to detach yourself enough to approach your descriptions more objectively. Writing in the third person can also result in more self-compassion, giving you a new lens on the impact of your brand impression.[4]

Step 4: Capture Your ID Visuals

Visuals often speak louder than words. As you create your Influence ID, what kind of image are you creating alongside your content pillars? You might be walking around with an expired ID photo that is over 10 years old and no longer resembles you at all. I get it—most of us do wish we looked 10 years younger and could use that photo forever. Who doesn't? But you do not want someone questioning if who they see online is actually you. We discount showcasing the experience and journey that comes with keeping our visuals updated, but it is a key point of differentiation we do not want to miss. Your visuals stand out first on your influence ID and online presence, so you must determine how you want your visuals to impact your brand.

Your ID has two types of images featured: images you can control and images you earn. At the top of your Influence ID are the images you can control. Think of these images as your online profile images that you place on your website or social media profiles. There are two important things to accomplish with this image—it should be a current reflection of you and showcase differentiation. For example, if you are an attorney and you have the typical suit and tie photo in front of a bookcase, you are doing nothing to differentiate yourself from other attorneys out there. With that standard photo, you have visually positioned yourself as a commodity online. Your goal with the visuals you control is to find an image of you in action to build credibility and differentiate yourself as a leader in your field. Simply, visuals have more impact on how differentiation is perceived than we think. If you have a photo in action interacting with clients, on a stage teaching others, or giving an interview, right or wrong, the perception of you shifts significantly. If you are deciding on your ID photo and you do not have any of those options currently available, intentionally look for opportunities to upgrade your photo as soon as possible to create the right first impression for your brand, which we will cover more in the next step.

Other images on your Influence ID are images you cannot necessarily control, but you can earn when invited onto someone else's platform.

These images are like passport stamps that other countries give your passport book to show you have credibly visited that country. Media, award organizations, and stages all give out visual passport stamps that you permanently should feature on your Influence ID. This showcases validation of the credibility you have earned with each opportunity and allows you to display these stamps for others to see how well-traveled you are. When you can present a Forbes logo, an Inc. 5000 award banner, or a photo of you on the TEDx stage, your ID credibility is further reinforced as the go-to expert in your industry.

You might be thinking this sounds like I'm asking you to brag about yourself to others. I assure you I intend to avoid that at all costs—Strategic Business Influencers are never in a position where they have to brag about themselves. I want you to use visuals on your ID to say what you won't say about yourself. Then you will have your content pillars and one-liner to establish your mission. The visual ID stamps you earn are credibility builders for you and showcase why someone should continue reading your content, meet with you, or take the next step to do business with you. It will take longer for trust and differentiation to be built if you are not leading with the visuals that will get them there quickly. In today's world, the amount of time we have to create an impression online is finite, so we have to be intentional in the visuals we select to add to our Influence ID to accelerate our credibility as quickly as possible.

Step 5: Craft Your One-Liner

Since your Influence ID is a one-page snapshot to get you in the door, you do have to find a quick way to present it concisely to gain access. Once you are granted access to your destination, you can build on pillars of your influence to create a greater impact, which is our next step. Step 5 in the process is kind of like crafting a corporate marketing tagline without all the traditional marketing rules. Since this is for your personal ID, you can make this one-liner really anything you want. Your ID one-liner can be a value statement, battle cry, or a short list of attributes. Some best practices are to keep the following in mind.

- Make it memorable.
- Keep it concise.
- Focus on value.
- Clarify differentiation.
- Simplicity wins.

Do not worry about getting clever with your ID one-liner. You are not trying to convey something new about yourself here. You are only trying to quickly give a snapshot of who you already are. Focus on your top two or three areas of differentiation to derive the best language to utilize in your one-liner. Below are examples from various industries.

- Guiding CEOs to achieve their dreams.
- Authentic Leadership. Bold Innovation.
- Resilient. Authentic. Unshakable.
- Take what's broken and make it better.
- Pioneering wellness through science and leadership.
- Lighting the way forward.

I encourage you not to overthink this step. It does not need to be sexy; it just needs to stick to the differentiation you identified in step 2. What you set today as your one-liner will not be what defines you for the next 25 years. In fact, it will change over time.

Cameron H. Block, our example entrepreneur who walked through each step of the Influence ID process, crafted the following one-liner to represent where he currently stands: "Simplifying supply chains to empower manufacturers and drive progress."

After you master these five steps, you are ready to receive your newly issued Influence ID. This one-page look will give you the credentials you need to gain access to future ventures, stages, media opportunities, and impact. When you put it all together, your final ID should mirror the image below.

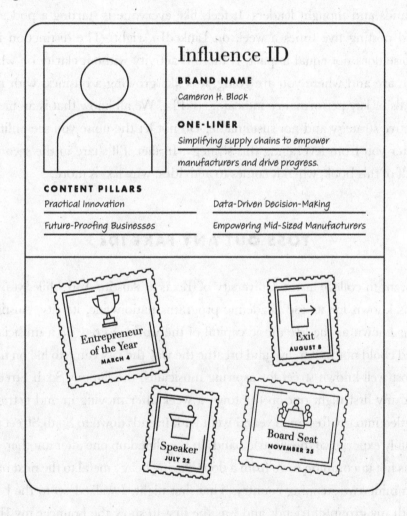

Once you are ready to take the next step and align your brand and goals to stand out in your field, download the Influence ID template where you can fill in each step of the process listed above to home in on your brand at paigevelasquezbudde.com. This exercise will set up your foundation for success and help you align your unique story with your business goals for maximum impact.

You might have been hesitant to get this far with your brand in the past, feeling like there is already a lot of noise from so-called personal brands and thought leaders. It feels like everyone is starting a podcast and posting five times a week on LinkedIn, right? The distinction is: Noise does not equal impact. If there is activity without clarity on who you are and where you are going, it is like growing a business with no goals or key performance indicators (KPIs). We all know that is an ineffective strategy and not sustainable. Do not let the noise you see online deter you from leveraging this strategy. In fact, I'll share in the second half of this book, when it comes to activities, why less is more.

TOSS OUT ANY FAKE IDs

I went to college at the University of Texas at Austin. And while, yes, it was known for its top academic programs nationwide, its city, Austin, was known as the live music capital of the world. I grew up a musician and could not wait to live and breathe the way the city came to life on the most well-known street for aspiring musicians, the famous Sixth Street. On my first night out on the town a week after moving in and getting settled into my freshman year, I went with friends down to Sixth Street to finally experience the electric bands in bars lined up one after another. It was not uncommon to go from a door blaring heavy metal to the next bar jamming two-stepping country. That first night, I walked up to the bar with my group of friends and was the first to show the bouncer my ID, only to get turned down. Turns out every bar on Sixth Street has an age restriction of 21 and up. Unfortunately, I had to stand outside to hear the band we went to see because I did not have the right credentials to gain access to the bar. So what did I do? I did what, at the time, I thought was the logical thing to do. I went to a dark basement in a building on West Campus where a fellow student had a one-stop shop to create a fake ID. Once I had that fake ID, I was barhopping all over Sixth Street before the age of 21. (If you are just now learning this, I'm sorry, Mom and Dad!) Did that fake ID give me access for a brief time? Yes. Did it look real? Not at all—that plastic was way too thick to be realistic. Did that access last forever? Nope. The gig was up when I was caught by a bouncer at The Blind Pig my sophomore year. Luckily, all he did was take the ID, cut it up, and throw it away. I was fortunate not to face more dire consequences.

Are there moments in life when you have encountered people trying to use a fake ID? The reality is that an inauthentic approach does not work. I do not want you to try to build an ID around something you are not. Not only will your audience know it because it will not come off as authentic, but it will exhaust you and not be a rewarding process. The energy it would take you to keep up with a fake ID will eventually catch up to you.

Some leaders who try to build visibility around their brand default to celebrity-like, personal branding tactics focused on creating a face for their business. This leads to a cheesy, overly promotional approach that turns an audience off. To be clear, Strategic Business Influencers have no personas or facades. Nor should you build "a face" for your company. That is a dated marketing tactic that leads with a sales pitch. Remember, these approaches no longer work. As a Strategic Business Influencer, you stand alongside your company, not in front of it or behind it. This is a visual alignment you must get right. Your Influence ID simply represents who you are with the right blend of information. You are doing nothing more than bringing visibility to the work you are already doing behind the scenes in your business every day. I want you to lean in on being more of yourself—that is what the Influence ID is really about. When you master articulating this, you open up your ability to scale your impact as a leader beyond your current team and customers.

YOU HAVE YOUR INFLUENCE ID—NOW WHAT?

Keep your ID on you at all times. Your Influence ID articulates your differentiation—if you keep it on you at all times, it will help you rise above the noise. Artificial intelligence has completely changed the landscape of marketing because it has increased accessibility for good content, graphic design, and consistency. It truly is amazing what you can produce with the right AI platform, and to be clear, I do not think all AI is bad. In fact, I believe AI serves a competitive advantage in the marketing field when you understand how to utilize it for efficiency, data analysis, brainstorming, and optimization. The challenge with AI currently is that people are now mass-producing content and saturating the market with a lot of noise. Some experts anticipate AI-generated content will make up to 90% of all online content in the near future.[5] Subconsciously, audiences are starting to glaze over the content information overload. If your marketing strategy relies on AI to churn out content for your brand, what is setting your content apart from your competitors? One of my favorite styles of music is country music, and because of my background in music, I love to keep up with the industry and discover new artists. There are a thousand radio stations, podcasts, or playlists I could listen to in order to get my country music fix. During my early years in Austin, I discovered a radio show called *The Bobby Bones Show*. Bobby and his cohosts not only gave me the latest in country music, but he also shared stories from the songwriters behind the music. Listening to his show made it feel like you were in a room with your friends versus the traditional hosts faking booming radio voices. A strong differentiator is that Bobby did not hire talent; he hired his friends on the show to keep the personality unique. This Influence ID for Bobby has put him on the map as a "different kind of country music morning radio show."[6] Leaning more into himself is what sets him apart. This same principle goes for people I follow for investment and health advice. It is not only about getting quality information; the influencers I pay attention to give me both information and perspective I cannot get anywhere else. So, when we think about utilizing AI to generate content for content's sake, it will not do anything to drive results for your business. Yes, AI can replace a corporate brand's voice, but it cannot replace what makes you authentically you.

As you carry your ID throughout the years, at some point, it will expire. Do not worry, what is written on your Influence ID is not set in stone; in fact, you will have to come back from time to time to renew it. You will need to update where you have been, where you are, and where you want to go. Career events like an exit, venture launch, name change, and new level of business all require the renewal process. For example, I met with a woman after a three-hour group workshop who had a strong Influence ID. She clearly articulated her credibility, mission, and vision throughout each of her online platforms. Her brand was built as a classic Strategic Business Influencer. Her concern after participating in the workshop was that, even though everything we reviewed created a strong differentiation for her brand, it was over three years old. This time span would typically not be a major issue, but she was about to go out for her first round of funding in four months' time. With a fast-growing business, a lot had changed for her over the past three years. This entrepreneur knew every potential investor she met with would be looking for a reason not to move forward with their investment, so she had to work quickly to renew her Influence ID to make sure her image mirrored what had been going on in her business. She only then would be able to confidently leverage her ID to secure those initial meetings.

When you meet these career and life milestones over time, go back to the five-step process to refresh the areas that need to be updated. I've seen many leaders who have tried to continue growth with an expired license because they did not take the time to make updates. This lack of attention creates conflicting first impressions, limits growth, and hinders perceived value. Updating your ID every few years will require much less energy than the first time around.

One morning, I was on the dreaded 5 AM flight from Austin to New York City for meetings. This meant I had to get to the airport by 3:30 AM, which further meant I had to leave my house no later than 2:45 AM. With a four-and-a-half-hour flight ahead of me and not enough coffee to muster the energy to go full glam at two o'clock in the morning, I decided to ditch the hair and makeup and do it on the plane. After arriving at the Austin airport, I walked into the CLEAR TSA PreCheck line to try and get through security as quickly as possible so I could have enough time to fuel my body with caffeine before boarding the plane. When I was called up to the CLEAR system's face scanner, I stared at the green dot and got back an error message. One of the workers came over and helped me rescan my face, and again, another error message. This happened three times before we resorted to the finger scan method. Once I got the green approved message, the screen displayed the picture I had taken when I did my CLEAR application. The worker then informed me, "Oh, that might be the issue. That picture does not look like you." Ouch. That was a tough one to hear before the sunrise.

The same scenario can happen when your Influence ID does not match the current image you actually have online. Once your ID is issued, it does not magically appear on all of your platforms. You have to intentionally examine your current image to find where your ID might not match up. You do not want anyone to question if you are who you say you are because you have not accurately reflected your Influence ID or, in my case, full glam at two in the morning. So, to avoid any mishaps, put your Influence ID into action so it can be leveraged to get you into the right doors. To help with that, I will share in this next step how to examine and update your current image across your online platforms to avoid any areas of misidentification.

Step 2

EVALUATE YOUR FIRST IMPRESSION

Your Influence ID is the foundation for a public-facing representation of who you are—the cornerstone of your brand as a Strategic Business Influencer, blending the credibility of where you have been with a clear vision for where you want to go. Now that your Influence ID has been issued, you have uncovered the most unique asset that will allow you to differentiate your business from your competitors. This is a massive milestone to reach as a Strategic Business Influencer because you have established the guiding light for your brand. This point in the process is where I tend to hear most entrepreneurs say, "Let's go! I'm ready to speak, create content, reach people, and get my brand out there." This is when I have to sit down and have the ready, fire, aim conversation. Although jumping to execution immediately to garner more brand visibility can yield short-term results, executing before the concrete on your foundation is dry will cause cracks that you will be working to patch for years to come.

So, before you start crafting a lengthy LinkedIn post to broadcast your thought leadership, pause. Although we are only in step 2, there is a reason the book does not get to marketing activity until step 4. I promise we will get there in due time. We must first lay the proper foundation by evaluating your current image online against your Influence ID to ensure the information is up-to-date and congruent.

Have you ever considered that the first image people create for you is not the first time you walk into a room or get on a Zoom call? It is created when people first search for you online. What they find in that online search sets a tone for how much they trust you or not ahead of a face-to-face interaction.

When somebody types your name into a search, what's the first thing they see? The results that populate at the top of that search on page 1 are what is currently painting the picture of your brand. Are the results that populate aligning with your Influence ID, or are there areas that reflect an old ID that needs to be renewed? The reality in today's society is a leader's first impression no longer happens in person. It's formed when a potential customer, investor, employee, or interested party searches a leader's name. As Rachel Greenwald wrote in *Harvard Business Review*, "The 'first' impression of you isn't when you actually make contact, it's when someone pulls up your internet profiles and makes snap judgments from their screen."[1] To build your brand as a Strategic Business Influencer, you have to step back and take a hard look at your current image and determine if it will accelerate or hold back your business.

HOW QUICKLY JUDGMENTS ARE MADE ONLINE

For most of us, society has instilled in us the importance of a first impression since grade school. It has become part of our innate nature to want people to like us after their first interaction. As leaders, we know the weight a strong first impression can have for our company's success, but more importantly, we understand the lasting damage a bad impression can have on an audience's mind.

When it comes to people, first impressions are formed within milliseconds of meeting someone,[2] and in that instant, judgments such as competence, trustworthiness, and likability are made. So you do everything you can to influence a positive experience for any meeting you take from your handshake, to what you wear, to the preparation of your conversation. What you must realize in today's environment is that your first impression is happening long before any of those things occur.

The advertising agency's creation can be dated back to the early 1800s. Advertising agencies have built businesses based on companies paying them to conduct research and formulate campaigns that center around one thing—creating and controlling the best first impression for the brand or product and growing brand loyalty from there. In today's world, well-known companies are more trusted by consumers because they have invested millions of dollars in advertising over several years. The need to compete on this level of brand recognition is why leaders pour much-needed time and resources throughout their entire entrepreneurial careers into perfecting their brand's tagline and brand colors, building the best company website, and coming up with the right activation strategies. To be clear, intentional branding and marketing are needed for a corporate brand. However, only focusing on your corporate brand's impression can result in a long timeline and high investment until you see results based on our current environment of corporate distrust.

If you are reading this book, odds are you do not have hundreds of millions of dollars to compete with large competitors in your industry to quickly create a stronger impression for your company, service, or product. So, how are you strategically going to win?

As the founder or leader of your company, you know that you must pound the pavement to get every opportunity for your company to grow and scale. So the first impression of you as the leader, or any executive representing your company, becomes just as important as your corporate brand's first impression. Many times, you personally will be encountered through business transactions before your corporate logo. That first impression as a leader can determine if someone trusts you with their investment and has the confidence to award you a contract or decides to leave their current job to come to work for you.

Your true first impression no longer happens in person at that meeting. Your first impression is now formed when someone searches your name on Google or an AI platform after seeing your email, calendar invite, or a peer recommends you. The hard truth is that no matter how well that meeting might go, you are going in with an impression (positive or negative) that will be challenging to combat because of the human nature of what happens when someone makes a snap judgment based on what they have seen during their initial research online. So, as leaders, we must realize our control of an interaction needs to start much earlier than we might think, and the focus needs to shift to what our personal, executive brand represents alongside our corporate brand. Decision-makers are always looking for a reason not to take a meeting, hire you, interview you, and so on. You must focus on controlling everything you can to avoid someone making the wrong snap judgment about you and your company.

Think about the first time you meet someone in person. There is a gut feeling that you either trust them or you don't. The science behind how quickly we make a judgment when it comes to first impressions is fascinating. It's all a gut reaction based on body language that we can't help but form upon the first interaction. Within seconds, a person is either validating your initial impression or they are climbing out of a hole with you internally to prove this reaction wrong, without their knowledge of it.

Online first impressions have quickly and overwhelmingly become the norm, with 75% of business meetings now conducted via videoconferencing.[3] With online being the primary place first impressions are formed today, recent studies show that it's now more than an image of the face that influences snap judgment. It matters what the visuals are in the background to determine if one is perceived as trustworthy.[4]

The same thing happens when we take 10 seconds on a quick Google search. Once someone lands on a web page, whether it's your company website or your LinkedIn page, an impression is formed within 50 milliseconds.[5]

Yes, a tenth of a second.

This statistic absolutely makes me want to pull out my hair, probably like most of you who have spent any time or resources on marketing or content strategy. The content we spend so much time on isn't the first impression. We utilize content to reinforce trust and accelerate education and our mission, and there is a need for strategic thinking here—which is why I spent a full chapter in part 2 of the book on it.

Although we spend time creating incredible content for our businesses, creative campaigns, and powerful press opportunities, the reality is most people will never get to the content unless they know you are the leader in your industry. They realistically aren't going to take the time to do this unless they know you are the person to teach them on this topic.

Think about how you have made snap judgments of other businesses or peers in the past without realizing it. Maybe you were referred to a business attorney, and you landed on their outdated website that looked like it was from the early 2000s with clip art imagery. You are trying to be innovative with your business, and your gut reaction was they would not be a fit because of their outdated thinking.

What about when you googled a CEO you were about to have lunch with because a peer introduced you via email to collaborate on opportunities? The second search that appeared under his name you could see was a negative Glassdoor review. That sentiment is now going to be in the back of your mind throughout that entire lunch. Was that reviewer on par with their comments, or were they just a disgruntled employee?

Whether we're meeting with a referral, interviewing a candidate, or looking up a product we heard about, we all form an impression of that initial search that is determined by what we find or what we don't find. So, how do we ensure we're forming an impression that creates trust for our brand?

THE INTERSECTION OF TRUST FOR CORPORATE BRANDING AND EXECUTIVE BRANDING

Like most entrepreneurs and leaders, you have probably spent countless years of time, sweat, resources, and, let's be honest, tears pouring into your business. Your relentless focus has been on creating the best product, building a world-class team, and establishing a reputable brand. That grind with your corporate brand is what got you here, but with the shifts we have seen in the consumer environment, leading your growth with a corporate brand alone is no longer enough. Why? Consumers are more skeptical of businesses and logos than ever. A Gallup study in 2022 showed that, over a 29-year study, the average confidence in US institutions across several categories of business, government, and schools significantly declined to an all-time low, presenting a confidence crisis.[6] This seismic shift in our society has pushed businesses into a defensive position upon first interaction versus a traditional offensive stance.

Since businesses no longer begin interactions with a foundation of trust, leaders are now forced to crack the code on how to take someone from skeptic to trusted follower. This is why the ability as a leader to build trust on behalf of your company is now a premium in business. PwC's 2024 trust survey underscored that business executives understood the importance of building trust, citing that it has increased the bottom line. What they uncovered, though, was that leaders and companies were blindly confident about trust levels with their consumers.

> **THE RESULTS SHOWED THAT 90% OF BUSINESS LEADERS BELIEVED CUSTOMERS TRUSTED THEIR COMPANY, BUT IN REALITY, ONLY 30% OF CONSUMERS DID.**[7]

As a leader, the conversation of declining confidence and trust in institutions has most likely been on your radar, but this 60-point trust gap is hopefully a wake-up call that traditional corporate marketing tactics are no longer working. To overcome this gap, leaders must be willing to step out from behind their businesses and build their executive brands on the front lines alongside their corporate brand. When building a business in today's environment, you are not only going to battle with your larger competitors, you are also fighting skepticism, confidence, and trust. As the leader, you need to put yourself in a position to lead the battle cry.

While creating a more visible executive brand might feel distracting and like it goes against everything you believe as a leader, what I hope you learn from this book is that I am not asking you to approach this in a self-serving way or focus on a lot of additional activities that will result in a time suck. In fact, I'm sharing how to focus your time on the highest-impact strategies that will bring the visibility of your impactful leadership to scale.

If you have an impactful message to get out and you are solely communicating it through your corporate brand, it will take a longer time period, cost more money, and be less effective at reaching your audience because there is a trust barrier for corporate brands. If you, as the leader, are willing to be that messenger—not the focused message—your impact will go further, be accelerated, and cost less. This is why I believe becoming a Strategic Business Influencer is imperative for small to medium-sized business owners.

THE INVISIBLE LEADER

I cannot tell you how often I've heard from entrepreneurs that being online "just isn't their thing." Most of them say they have intentionally tried to be a ghost online because they were uncomfortable putting themselves out there or did not want to come across as self-promotional. I believe these are both valid concerns many leaders wrestle with. If this is how you feel, I want to ease your concerns. Becoming a Strategic Business Influencer will help you overcome these challenges while keeping your humility fully intact. The truth is, it is almost impossible for today's leaders to be a ghost online. With the accessibility of the internet and social media, your brand as an executive is most likely visible whether you like it or not. The question becomes, are you taking action to control the image that is created of you online, or are you letting others dictate your image by leaving it untouched? Even if you're not active online, you *are* online—it just means others own your first impression instead of you. I want to help you change that with this book.

I have traveled to leadership conferences around the world to conduct what I call one-on-one executive brand audits. During these audit sessions, I sit down with CEOs for 15 minutes at a time to evaluate their image and give actionable feedback to enhance their first impression online and build trust on behalf of their business. I sat down with an entrepreneur at an event in New York City, and he started off the session with the comment that he had "intentionally been good at keeping his executive brand offline" and assured me I would only need to audit his corporate brand assets. I went ahead and analyzed his company website, social media profiles, review websites, and press strategy. His corporate brand was in pretty good shape, but he mentioned he was about to raise his next round of capital, so I gave him a few thoughts to take back to his marketing team to enhance their content strategy. Before he got up from the table, I asked if he would mind staying a few minutes longer for one more thing.

I wanted to see what would happen if I put myself in the mind of a potential investor, so I googled his name. This is exactly what every potential investor for his company will do before walking into a meeting—or perhaps even before deciding whether or not to take the meeting in the first place. They will want to know who they are meeting with and gather as much information as possible before walking into the meeting room. To this leader's surprise, thousands of results populated when I typed in his name into Google. Several of the first links were to posts on social media platforms mentioning him at events, and even one post that featured a photo of him speaking. There was also an eight-year-old YouTube interview video populating the top results, which he begged me not to click on so he did not have to go through the agony of watching the poorly produced video again.

As we were walking through the search results, I shared my concern with him that he *does* have an online presence; it is just out of his control. Currently, an investor will find what everyone else has taken the time to post online about him, not the image he wants to reinforce in his pitch to them. The saying about your competitors that "while you are sleeping, someone else is grinding" is true when it comes to your discoverability online as well. If you are sleeping on your online presence because you think you do not need it or it is not your thing, you are losing. With the shifting behaviors online, someone is grinding to become the go-to expert in your field, or worse, someone else is controlling your image. If no one can find how to access you online, you will continue to lose out on opportunities.

There is a significant risk if you do not take control of your image online because someone will always be there, ready to take control of it for you. This is a step in the process you want to remain proactive with to maintain as much control as possible and align your current image with your Influence ID to create the best first impression for you and your business.

CONDUCTING YOUR EXECUTIVE BRAND AUDIT

To begin your image evaluation, I will walk you through conducting an executive brand audit to identify the areas of your online presence that need revising to match your newly issued Influence ID. Throughout the exercise, I encourage you to think like a prospect doing their research before entering the discovery meeting.

The scenario I want to draw up is this prospect you are envisioning was referred to you by a longtime client you have done work with for years. This prospect was given your name and phone number as the main point of contact. Before the prospect picks up the phone to give you a call, they will search your name to make sure what shows up matches all the great stuff they were told about you. The first question I want you to ask yourself in this scenario is: Can you be found once I search your name on Google or an AI platform?

Some leaders are trying to build an executive brand with a first and last name so common that it is almost impossible to rank on page 1 of Google or come up as the first line of information on an AI platform search. If you have a common name or share your name with a well-known athlete, they have most likely built up all of the clout around that brand, making it exceedingly difficult to be discoverable without paying for it. Even then, depending on the name, you most likely will not be able to sustain a paid strategy approach. So, if you find yourself in this conundrum, I want you to consider changing your name.

Cue the record scratch!

To be clear, I do not plan on putting you through a deep branding exercise to develop a completely new name. I'm only asking you to make a small shift in your name, like adding your middle name or middle initial to your executive brand. Once you add this element, you are creating clear differentiation away from those commonalities, and you can organically be discoverable. Think about how hard it is to generate a referral or enough interest that someone is looking for you by name.

Don't you want to make it easy for them to find you?

For example, I met with serial entrepreneur Jason P. Carroll to work through his brand discovery crisis under the search phrase "Jason Carroll." On top of it being an incredibly common name, there was also a nationally recognized CNN journalist with the same name dominating most of the page-1 searches. Jason researched a few variations of his name and ultimately landed on adding his middle initial to his brand name to establish clear credibility as he prepared to launch his new venture, Aptive Index. When changing your name, do not confuse this as a stage name you need to get creative with. This shift should be a practical decision on what is most discoverable for your brand name. Avoid any gimmicks that can cause you to not be taken seriously, even if you are not thrilled about that middle name.

Another example is the iconic actor Michael J. Fox. Early in his career, he realized the name Michael Fox was already reserved by an actor in the Screen Actors Guild. He added the initial J to his brand name to pay homage to his favorite actor, Michael J. Pollard. Adding this middle initial allowed him to quickly differentiate himself as he began building his career. This one small shift can determine whether your brand is discoverable. If you have to change your name, ensure you immediately change all the assets you can so you are not piecemealing your brand together.

Other reasons you might need to change your name include a life event like a marriage or divorce. I speak with many women who go through life events and find that a name change can potentially disrupt discoverability around an image they have been curating for years. Several years ago, I had to face this change myself when I got married. I was excited to embrace my husband's last name, only to realize I had built my career's online presence around the brand name Paige Velasquez. If

I had shifted entirely to my new name, Paige Budde, my brand image would have been erased because none of my past website features or press hits would have populated under that search term. This led to the decision to tack on my new last name to my maiden name, which I had built up favorable search engine optimization (SEO) around for years. This allowed my search results to continue to populate under the recognized phrase Paige Velasquez while building fresh results under Paige Velasquez Budde. While changing your name for marriage can be an easy fix if you know how to do it right, changing it after a divorce can be complex and challenging. I have sat down with some women who have ultimately decided to keep their married name after a divorce because too much had been built up throughout their careers under their brand name to let it go now. Others have been able to easily drop their married last name if they included a maiden name and married last name in their brand name. If you are in a dire situation where you need to make a complete shift in your last name, just know it might take time to populate your image with the results you want to serve as your first impression. The key is to make the name change cohesive across all assets you can control, such as your website, social media platforms, Google listings, videos, review websites, and so on. It will take time, but those assets will eventually populate under your changed name. The only thing you might lose is past media stories that you cannot change using your previous name.

Once your executive brand name is established, you must protect your discoverability and ownership of your name at all costs. One of the best ways to do this is by reserving your brand name, FirstNameLastName.com, as a website URL. You can go to any domain register, such as GoDaddy, and purchase your name as a website URL for an average of $12 per year. It is a pretty low cost to prevent others from controlling your image, right? I know you might be recoiling against the idea of building a personal website around your brand name. We will address if and when you should consider this as a Strategic Business Influencer, but to ease your fears, a personal website does not make sense for everyone. Whether you plan to build a website or not, buying your domain name forms a hedge of protection around your executive brand. Your URL is one of the most precious assets in the digital world today.

As you evaluate your discoverability, I would encourage you to also audit your company's name during this process. Is it a discoverable name, or is it so common that it is getting lost on page 10 of Google? If you are starting a new venture, run a quick Google and AI platform search on the brand names you are considering. Is the name easily discoverable? Meaning nothing is dominating the top search results consistently under that brand name? Doing this on the front end could save you a lot of time, money, and headache, realizing you have built a business with a brand name you will always be fighting a discoverability battle with.

Once you have established that your brand is discoverable, you now need to turn your attention to the links populating at the top of page 1 when you google your name and read what the AI search is saying about you. SEO experts Backlinko shared in their analysis of over four million Google search results that the top three results get over half of the clicks.[8] Knowing that's where a prospect will most likely click when searching your name, take the time to evaluate the top three results carefully, looking for any red flags that could work against you.

To ensure you are simulating the results someone will see when googling you for the first time, conduct your search on a private or incognito browser. That will ensure it's not pulling location, past search, or web history. Evaluate how many of the results you can control on page 1. Then ask yourself, am I doing everything I can to accelerate trust for me and my business?

When assessing your discoverability, it's important to know your digital leadership presence is now also driving discoverability for your company when it comes to informing AI platform discoverability and traditional search engine optimization. SEO pioneer and content expert Chris Kirksey, founder and CEO of Direction.com, shared the following about the importance of digital leadership visibility for today's companies.

True brand discoverability comes from credibility, connection, and conversion—in exactly that order. Google and Generative AI search engines heavily weigh expertise and authority in rankings. Their algorithms recognize and reward unique content that generates engagement. Thought leadership content sees longer time-on-page, higher engagement metrics, and three to four more times backlinks, shares, and mentions—all key factors in both organic search rankings and getting found in AI search systems such as ChatGPT and Perplexity, which are now more utilized than Bing. Search engines crave authority; AI demands credibility. Thought leadership delivers both.[9]

This is a significant shift we are seeing from legacy SEO, advertising, and marketing strategies with the way search and AI platforms are ranking brand authority that reaffirms the importance of a leader's role when it comes to building trust and credibility in today's environment.

WHAT BUILDS TRUST WHEN IT COMES TO YOUR FIRST IMPRESSION

Trust online starts with visuals and is then reinforced with content. This first starts with how you portray your brand's visuals and then focuses on how you leverage visuals associated with your brand.

If you are hoping that what you have out there with your company's corporate assets, such as your website and social media channels, are doing enough to build trust, they are not. As I mentioned earlier, it is exceedingly hard to gain trust with a corporate logo alone because people are skeptical when they just see a company pushing products or selling services. At the end of the day, people trust people. So it is in your best interests to have your brand (and maybe a few key executives) visible alongside the corporate brand.

One simple way to make your people more visible is to find ways to integrate photos of them on your corporate assets. If you land on your website home page and you have filled your website imagery with stock photos, you are immediately at a disadvantage because the odds are that the user has seen that photo on another website prior and cannot distinguish you from one company to another. Just like an Instagram feed, you know what photos are highly produced and unrealistic versus authentic photos of your team, facilities, and leaders. Studies have shown that photos that are more authentic than stock images get more engagement online.[10] That's because people can see through what is real and what is not. Think of every visual on your corporate and personal assets as an opportunity to differentiate your brand and showcase the experience a customer will have with you. There is no way to do that unless you control the imagery you associate with your brand as much as possible. The time and investment it takes to do this will pay off when you focus on presenting your brand as real and as authentic as possible.

Another way to establish trust online is to leverage visuals you can associate with your brand. For example, when I was five months into motherhood, we had hit the milestone to start incorporating solid foods into our baby's diet. As I started researching the food groups to introduce my son to first, I came across horrific new stories about heavy metals being found in various baby food brands on store shelves. It was at that moment I had the bright idea that I would circumvent that concern by preparing all of his baby food at home. I proudly went to the store every Sunday and purchased organic fruits and vegetables to meal prep my son's purees for the week. It was only two months later, when the doctor encouraged more variety in his diet, that my master plan all came crumbling down. At that point, I had to give in and realize I could not keep up with my meal prep to provide the various types of food he needed to explore. As a first-time parent, I was scared out of my mind to feed my baby something that could potentially harm him, but the reality was I needed to find another solution fast. I knew I could not be the only parent who faced this challenge, so I went to Google and searched the term "heavy metal–tested baby food." One of the first websites that populated was the Clean Label Project. It listed 11 brands that passed their rigorous product testing. As I clicked through the websites, each company had beautiful branding and bold statements about their clean product. There was one brand, Little Spoon, that stood out to me at first glance. As I landed on their website, they not only had beautiful product imagery and a well-structured tagline, but they also had images of media logos that I recognized with quotes about the product from each one. When I saw *Fast Company*, *Good Housekeeping*, and *Parents* on the page, there was a familiarity and subconscious positive perception shift that kept me scrolling, leading me to 30 minutes of research and, at the end of the journey, a purchased subscription.

You might have made a similar association in the past, whether it was with a potential company you were looking to hire or the right baby food for your infant. This type of association might have led you to reach out because you saw a company had won awards such as Inc. 5000, had impressive clients they represented, or were featured in media outlets you trust. This is why I believe finding known logos you can associate with your brand visually can help create credibility for your brand subconsciously in the minds of your audience. As you can see in the Little Spoon example above, this strategy also helps differentiate you from your competitors.

If you are just starting on the path of growing your visibility and you are not sure what imagery or logos you could associate with your brand, I want you to consider the type of business opportunities you are seeking for the future. For example, if recruiting talent is your top priority for the year, lead with company culture or growth awards like Best Places to Work or Fastest Growing Companies. If you are a B2B business looking to bring on more enterprise accounts, the logos you might lead with in that case are industry leadership awards or your WBENC certification. Think through what past experiences you have that most relate to the opportunities you are pursuing. It might be a past press logo, award, notable client, or event photo. I want you to associate those images with your brand across your platforms. The simple tactic of switching out your standard blue connecting dot LinkedIn cover image to a photo of you speaking on a stage or adding a credentialing logo to your website hero image is incredibly impactful when it comes to a first impression. Although it is not completely logical, there is a completely different perception of you as a leader that happens with that one minor tweak.

As you scale your company, you will naturally acquire more impactful imagery to feature, including bigger stages, more high-caliber logos, or more recognizable clients. Be mindful of capturing these opportunities and be steadfast in keeping your image updated. I see too many business owners who set it and forget it. When doing that, you are not maximizing the time, energy, and resources you put into these opportunities to attract more growth.

Now, at this point, some of you reading this might be starting to get a little uncomfortable or feeling that internal recoil that I mentioned earlier. You are probably thinking this feels pretty showy and could come off as egotistical. Most of us are humble leaders, and this feels like we are heading in a direction the complete opposite of that, right? If you have that fear, I promise that is a good sign. If you think this way as you become a Strategic Business Influencer, you will continue to stay mission-minded and build your brand in a way that will benefit your business long term.

The way to think about this strategy when it comes to visuals is . . .

I want you to envision yourself walking a tightrope. On one side of the rope, you have experienced credibility that needs to be visible to advance your first impression for the right opportunities. You can't lean too much to this side, or you will become overly promotional and turn your audience off. On the other side of the rope, you must focus on delivering value, education, and entertainment. But if you lean only to this side of the rope, no one may ever see your content, to begin with, or stay long enough to learn more about you if you do not know you are the person in a position to teach them about your area of expertise.

Think of it this way—you want the visuals to speak volumes and affirm that you are the leader in your industry without you ever having to say it. Then you want your content to bring forward your mission, teaching, and vision. I see so many businesses that have powerful content, but their audience growth is slower, and their sales cycle is longer than it needs to be. The more strategic approach is to put the right visuals in place to accelerate the first impression and, from there, spend your entire customer journey delivering valuable content you will continue to serve to them.

AUDITING YOUR WEBSITE, SOCIAL MEDIA PLATFORMS, AND PRESS

There are three common categories that could populate for a leader at the top of page 1 of Google search results: your website, social media platforms, or press. Let's break down how to spot potential red flags on each platform and what to do about them.

Additional Website Red Flags

My hope is that you either have a company website or personal website ranking in the top three results on a search for your name. A website is the most valuable home base you have in the digital landscape because it is the one platform you can control the entire image of. You get to make every decision, from design to user journey and content, of how you and your company are presented. If you do have a website, personal or corporate, and it is already ranking in the top three results, you have passed the first test. As you comb through your website, look to avoid the following.

- **Inconsistency with your executive brand name.** If you are utilizing a middle initial or a middle name, ensure it's displayed cohesively throughout the site. This is not only important for brand cohesiveness; it is critical to enhancing your SEO and maintaining your Google ranking.

- **Dated imagery.** Visuals on your website should be evaluated and updated, at a minimum, annually. I've sat down with many leaders who do not even want me to pull up their website because the last time they updated it was five years ago, and it does not reflect the caliber of work they now do. If you as the leader do not believe your website visuals position you as the best in the field, why would a prospect believe you are the industry leader?

- **First-person biography.** There was a wave of time when some marketers pushed the first-person written biography on LinkedIn profiles and business websites. The argument was a third-person biography read as cold and unapproachable. The challenge with this theory is that it led to first-person biographies coming off as self-promotional and salesy—two red flags you want to stay away from as a Strategic Business Influencer. Your website professional biography should be written in the third person, consist of 500 to 800 words, and balance your professional accomplishments with your missional impact. When well written, your biography should come across as credible, warm, and memorable. Utilizing your executive brand name when referring to yourself in your third-person biography will also enhance SEO for the website around your name.

- **All logo, no people.** This is the biggest red flag to look for as you review your website. We know traditional marketing of logos and corporate entities no longer gains trust for companies. If your leaders and people are invisible on your website, you are making it harder for customers, employees, partners, and investors to trust you.

What If Your Website Isn't Discoverable?

Now, let's address what to do if your company website is not ranking in the top three search results for your executive brand name. If you find yourself in this conundrum, it is most likely due to an SEO indexing issue for your brand name. To increase the chances of your website ranking high for your executive brand name, create a single page on your website that houses your brand name, photo, professional biography, and potentially a link to your LinkedIn page. For example, this page could have the URL www.company.com/about/firstnamelastname. If you have a pop-up for your biography or a drop-down within an About page on your website, this does not give SEO strength around your name. Google will give more weight to pages that are built solely around your brand name. I know this might seem overly tactical, but this shift will be a game changer when it comes to your website ranking.

Social Media Red Flags

While you cannot control the sections that make up your social media profiles, you do have control over how each section is presented for your brand. Since LinkedIn typically ranks in the top search results for most leaders, I am going to spend our time reviewing what to be on the lookout for when evaluating your LinkedIn profile image. Most of these red flags will be applicable to any other social media profiles you might have.

- **A default cover image.** The cover image on LinkedIn is the first horizontal image at the top of your profile someone sees when they land on your page. LinkedIn gives you this feature as an opportunity to visually establish your image quickly with anyone reviewing your profile. If you have not taken the time to be intentional about this image, you are missing a massive opportunity to convey your Influence ID. Your LinkedIn cover photo should quickly build credibility and differentiate you as a leader in your industry.

- **The picturesque cover image.** Whether it is a beach sunset, city skyline, or mountainscape, although beautiful, this image is doing nothing for you. As you evaluate your image, ask yourself, how is this visual building confidence for my brand? Consider swapping your nature photo with a shot of you giving an interview, speaking on a stage, a graphic of media logos you have been featured in or awards you have won. You want the visuals to convey a strong tone while the content of your profile focuses on providing pure value.

- **A difficult-to-recognize profile image.** Avoid having a low-resolution, cropped, or dated photo of yourself as your profile image. Opt for a high-quality up-close image you want to convey.

- **Inconsistency with your brand name.** Do a quick check to ensure your name on your LinkedIn profile is consistent with the executive brand name you are building discovery for. LinkedIn can be tricky with a middle initial or middle name because when you create your profile, there are only fields for a first name, last name, or additional name. If you have a middle initial or middle name, you will want to include it in the first name field to display it correctly on your profile.

- **The wordy headline.** The beauty and challenge with LinkedIn profiles is they are restricted to a 220-character limit. I see a lot of LinkedIn profiles that try to get philosophical or cutesy with their headline and waste opportunities to enhance their discoverability within the LinkedIn platform. Your headline is indexed for searchability and displayed next to your name across the platform, so you want to leverage it to convey aspects of your Influence ID quickly. Since you have a short character limit, your goal is to be as descriptive and credentialed as possible. You can pack a lot into 220 words. For example: Founder of Value Solutions | TEDx Speaker | Bestselling author | Inc. 5000 | EY Entrepreneur of the Year finalist.

- **An About section that is a sales pitch.** Similar to your website biography, you want to avoid having an About section that reads as if you are pitching yourself. That puts you in the position of leading with something to sell versus showcasing yourself as someone with something to teach. This approach goes against the grain of positioning yourself as a Strategic Business Influencer and can turn your audience off. In your LinkedIn About section, stick with a 500-word third-person professional biography.

- **The auto-populated LinkedIn URL.** When you click on your LinkedIn profile, look at the top of your browser and examine the URL. Typically, it will auto-generate your name in the URL, followed by a lot of letters and numbers. Edit your custom URL at the top right of your profile to get rid of all the letters and numbers and simply display, linkedin.com/in/firstnamelastname. This will ease the ability to display your

LinkedIn profile in your email signature and business cards and secure the ownership of your name on the platform.

Press Red Flags

Press can be a strong credentialing factor for your brand search results only if it reflects the image that aligns with your Influence ID. There is nothing more frustrating than when you conduct your Google search and one of the top three results is a link to an interview you did 10 years ago that makes you cringe because it does not accurately reflect who you are today. In fact, in some scenarios, those old interviews can do more harm than good if that is the first thing a prospect encounters. The challenge with press is you have no control over editing what is in that piece; the media outlet does. Unfortunately, fixing this will take a little time and an intentional PR strategy. Your best tactic is to focus on garnering new press opportunities to eventually outrank the old ones, which we will cover in step 6. Since that specific outlet has covered you before, you can even reach out with an idea for an updated story to align the image of you in that outlet with your Influence ID.

Additional Red Flags to Be on the Lookout For

As you review your search results, if you see a lot of dated assets that are no longer serving your brand, go ahead and take them down. That might mean you have to uncover the password to your old Twitter account so that your X profile you have not posted on in eight years is not the first thing a prospect sees. Maybe you need to delete old videos off of your YouTube channel that your team talked you into filming 10 years ago that are no longer on par with the quality of your brand. Your goal in this audit is to revise, remove, or outrank any result that does not align with your Influence ID or could be a liability to your brand.

LOOKING AT THE BIG PICTURE OF YOUR IMAGE

Conducting your executive brand audit is an extremely tactical exercise, but each step is crucial to ensuring your online image is in alignment with your Influence ID. Intentionality with your image online will build a rock-solid foundation to raise the visibility of your executive brand from behind your corporate logo to alongside it. Once you are in this position, it will give you leverage to create quick and impactful differentiation for your business.

Put yourself in the shoes of someone who has been referred to you—is what they find on a Google search going to reinforce the wisdom of that referral or cause them to question it?

As you reflect on what Google is currently saying about you, I want you to ask yourself if your current image is positioning you as an industry leader or another commodity. If your leadership has no visibility alongside your corporate brand, you are making it a lot harder on yourself to win in this business environment. If you continue to try and compete with a marketing strategy that goes logo versus logo alone, you will always find yourself as the underdog against your larger competitors. Some of the smartest Strategic Business Influencers I know are building their businesses with this need for differentiation in mind.

When entrepreneur Jason P. Carroll, whom I mentioned earlier in this chapter, called me about a new venture he was starting called Aptive Index, a psychometric assessment software company for workplace performance, he mentioned there was a lot of well-known competition already in the marketplace that had been dominating for decades. Yes, his software had the most advanced science and the slickest user experience. He knew, though, that leading with the brand name or product features would take a while to move the needle in the marketplace because his well-known competitor had thousands selling their product and logo in their sales force. This is why Jason called me ahead of his product launch. He knew that, to compete against the giants, he had to lead with what his competitors did not have—his story and personal experience sitting in the driver's seat of a rapidly growing organization. Jason had the experience of being at the helm of a company that he grew from 800 to over 2,500 employees in just seven years. He understood how costly it could be for leaders to make the wrong hire and have people in the wrong seats. After positioning the company for a successful exit, his entire personal life turned upside down and he found himself at a moment of deep reflection of "self-unawareness" that spurred the idea for Aptive Index. Jason knew he could open doors and garner more visibility by sharing the story that led him to launch Aptive Index rather than the product's list of flashy features. Since he knew educating other leaders on his lessons learned would kick-start the launch of Aptive Index, Jason decided it was time to not only evaluate his image but determine if the results that came up on Google conveyed the right first impression with leaders to encourage them to reach out to learn more about Aptive Index. What he found led to a full 180-degree shift to establish the right first impression with his new target audience. Now, when Jason googles "Jason P. Carroll," he dominates image control of every single page-1 result—which was not the result when we did his initial brand audit.

DIFFERENTIATING A RAW
MATERIALS MANUFACTURER

Naturally, some industries or brands might feel like they are better suited for a strong visual brand to build trust. For example, with a food company like Little Spoon, there is a lot of visual opportunity to differentiate a brand. What if your company is not in an industry as visual as baby food? Or maybe you believe your industry is too old school for this strategy. That assumption is false—the visual approach to your first impression is just as critical to your business no matter the industry.

I met award-winning entrepreneur Megan Gluth through the Women Presidents Organization in 2023. She was the CEO of a 30-year-old multinational raw material supplier and manufacturer at the time named TRInternational. Her story as the leader of TRInternational looked like an ideal climb of the corporate ladder. She joined the team as the company's first general counsel in 2012, then expanded her leadership over the years to president and advanced to the CEO role in 2018, and then completed her purchase of the company to become the sole owner and CEO in 2021. They became the largest women-owned suppliers of raw materials for North America, and in 2023, she was named a winner of EY's Entrepreneur of the Year, a coveted honor for any entrepreneur.

Although her story seemed to many like it had been what some would call an "overnight success," her true story as a leader was anything but that. Raised by a single mother in a rural town in northeast Iowa, Megan grappled with the harsh realities of poverty throughout her childhood. Alcohol abuse was a common coping mechanism in her community, and Megan herself turned to alcohol as an outlet during her college years.

Despite the challenges, Megan graduated from the University of Minnesota with a degree in history and was determined to pursue a career that would ensure her financial future. She took the LSAT exam and was accepted to law school at the University of St. Thomas. When she found herself short on tuition funds, a friend's father offered to cosign a loan for her. He always told himself that when he got to the place where he could help others, he would. He asked Megan to do the same. His compassion and belief in her potential affected Megan profoundly. The experience serves as inspiration for her "help others rise" leadership approach and support of her team members' career development.

Megan met her first wife in law school but lost her to cancer soon after passing the bar exam. Her grief sparked a renewed descent into alcoholism, which continued until those closest to her encouraged her to seek help. This wake-up call marked a turning point in Megan's life. She embraced self-accountability, and today, she is celebrating more than a decade of sobriety.

Megan used her battle with adversity to grow her leadership and differentiate her business from others in a traditional industry and long-standing company. She utilized her story and leadership to not only achieve outstanding business success but also create a profound cultural shift. She prioritized creating an atmosphere of excellence, accountability, and empathy within her company.

As she told her story to those closest to her and continued to grow the success of the company, many encouraged her to share her story more widely to inspire others to overcome challenging circumstances and find their own path to success:

I have had a thousand conversations with people where I shared my story, and then all of a sudden they say something like, "You don't know this about me, but I am struggling right now because I have a kid who is facing drug addiction." It is incredible what people tell me when I open up about my story. All of a sudden, you realize we are all carrying around real stuff we are facing that people are not talking about. We might think some people look like they have it all together, but they sometimes don't, and at the same time, they do. There is a level playing field when we open up human to human. When you are authentic, the difference between you and someone else, in reality . . . is nothing. You can only get this kind of connection through a person, not a company.[11]

Megan was clear on her vision for the company and her impact. She was on a path to grow the company and successfully acquire companies to expand the team's capabilities and services and ultimately bring all services under one roof with a rebrand to look to the future. As she prepared to take the next steps toward her vision of the company, she also knew it was time to step out alongside the company and tell her story to inspire others to overcome challenging circumstances and find their paths to success:

> *I realized by putting my brand out there, not everybody's gonna like me or my story. But that's also real life, right? I'm not building my brand to make me a likable celebrity to everyone who ever comes in contact with it. I am building my brand to put me in a place of accessibility for people who need what I have. Those people in my target audience are more trusting and they become more willing to engage. I would not have the opportunity to engage at this level if my brand was not out there for that point of accessibility.* [12]

As Megan built her brand as a Strategic Business Influencer, her company worked to finalize acquisitions and rebrand all three companies under a new umbrella, Catalynt. Megan's first impression online was extremely important as she began the acquisition process. She had to create the right first impression for any business owner, board member, or potential employee googling her ahead of a meeting. From her LinkedIn to her personal website, Megan's channels underwent a complete make-over to share her proven leadership, story, and authentic heart. Once her foundational online elements were established, she began doing select media opportunities and telling her story in outlets like The Business Journals, Authority Magazine, and podcasts like *What's Your "And"?*. The goal was to make the leadership she had every day in her company more visible at scale:

> *Everyone who deals with me in business knows what you see is what you get. I intentionally set up my online presence to reflect this as well. We didn't put any lipstick on a pig, as we would say in the Midwest, when it came to building my brand online. There is not anything fake about it. This type of*

first impression online has helped with business because, at the end of the day, business comes down to trust. Especially when in acquisition conversations, everything goes away, we don't trust one another. I know people google me before they take a meeting, and what they see of my brand online helps. They know what they are going to get. When I walk into a room, and I am exactly who they saw online, the brand itself becomes more credible.[13]

Her corporate marketing team worked for months on the company's rebrand, ensuring it encapsulated the merging of companies but, more importantly, the focus of the vision for the future. When Catalynt launched, the team not only had an upgraded logo, color scheme, and brand messaging that put them miles ahead of others in their industry, but they also utilized real photos of their team throughout the website and imagery online. This type of imagery was not standard for their industry and immediately resulted in clear differentiation for their company.

In addition to the upgraded visuals when you land on Catalynt's website and social media channels, their SEO (search engine optimization) also shifted. Search for both Megan and Catalynt points to not only the differentiating foundational assets, it also showcases the interviews with Megan, where she dove into her story and mission behind Catalynt. This first impression is now painting a completely different picture than before 2023 and draws a clear distinction for her company in the manufacturing industry. It's also creating a legacy for Megan to inspire others to overcome challenging circumstances and find their paths to success:

I have realized that people are never going to agree 100% with the decisions you make. The power in building my brand is I have the opportunity to control that narrative. I believe that benefits business relationships and my relationships with employees. My accessibility is greater, so they now know more about how I think, and I have an opportunity to share more about why I make certain decisions. I find there is more alignment all around with my brand alongside the company. I have actually been surprised with how easy this process is when staying authentic to myself.[14]

My hope is that Megan's story encourages you, no matter what industry you're in, to focus on the impact your first impression can have on your business and beyond. With everyone having search at their fingertips, the accessibility to access leaders is greater than ever. From Fortune 100 CEOs to small business owners, everyone has access to the same online platforms, leveling out the vast playing field of business. If you can play on the same field as your direct competitors, why would you not put your best impression forward and shine in areas they are not? Strategically capitalizing on the most unique asset in your business, your leadership, allows you to create a differentiator that cannot be replicated by your competition.

WHAT DOES AI SAY ABOUT YOU?

It is no surprise that AI is disrupting the search landscape. Traditionally, most searches have occurred on Google, but as AI platforms become more integrated into daily life, younger generations are now more likely to use AI platforms as search engines.[15] Gartner predicts search engine volume will drop by 25% in the coming years, losing its share to AI platforms and bots.[16] As you gather data on your first impression, you also want to uncover what AI says about you. Many AI platforms are driven less by keywords and more by user search intent. A search engine optimization keyword strategy focuses on including specific words or phrases people use to search for information online. User search intent is a strategy that narrows in on the purpose of the search, such as learning something or making a purchase. This shift allows for AI to provide more personalized results and humanlike experiences. Open up ChatGPT and simply ask it what it knows about yourself and your company. What web pages is it pulling from? Are there updates you need to make to those pages to feed ChatGPT the right information?

In 2023, I was in a room with over 20 executives at our Austin Women Presidents Organization monthly meeting. We'd just finished a session learning more about the future of AI and how we could strategically integrate it into our businesses. After the presentation, we had an open discussion of how we were currently experimenting with or utilizing AI in our businesses, but it was not until one of the women asked the group a simple question that I realized there was about to be an entirely new element introduced to searchability and discoverability online.

She simply asked the group a few simple questions: "Have you ever asked ChatGPT about yourself or your company? What if I asked about the market leader in your industry? Can we ask ChatGPT how we should integrate AI into our businesses?" Now, this was before Google introduced its AI Overview or any of the social media channels had integrated AI search into their platforms, so not many people had AI integrated into their searches without seeking out a specific AI platform. Now, things are vastly different, and AI has been more heavily integrated into our daily platforms, such as Google, LinkedIn, and email. Statistics have also shown that AI search is now becoming the first destination people will go to when seeking out information.[17] So, if you are not paying attention to your first impression on a generative AI search platform, you are missing a critical opportunity for you and your company.

With the introduction of Search Generative Experience (SGE), Google can now give users relevant answers to specific long-tail SEO questions. Google has introduced RankBrain as its AI algorithm and is utilizing AI to provide an overview of web pages and highlight key points relevant to the question to give information to users in a more digestible format. This allows users to get exactly what they are looking for without having to click on every web page. It's a very powerful tool to accelerate research or affirm credibility, but concerning if you have not paid attention to how your brand is faring in these searches. Without getting too technical, SGE has introduced the importance of user search intent. Before RankBrain, Google would only match up exact keywords searched with indexed web pages sharing those exact keywords.

Your discoverability is now less about a few keywords and more about the description of images, understanding your audience's user intent, and personalizing your meaning and value. Are you missing out on opportunities because you do not come up on a Search Generative Experience or is it not pulling the information to form the best first impression?

Algorithms are now also looking at how long users stay on your website, the amount of traffic you are getting, and if you are answering questions people typically search for throughout your content. The ability to create the right first impression and keep people scrolling because they know you are an industry leader will enhance your probability of being featured in an SGE search. The gravity of mastering SGE and SEO for you and your business is great as AI continues to advance. Right now, SGE searches are the very first thing that appears on most Google search results. Remember what we said about a first impression being created in milliseconds?

We have to keep a pulse on how search is evolving over time. It's going to be fully AI-driven, which means user intent when searching will become a lot more important. With AI-driven search rapidly growing, how do you control what populates when someone inputs your name? With AI, it is all about playing on offense; it can be really challenging to mitigate if you find yourself doing damage control. Below are the top activities that can influence and protect how AI talks about you (because, yes, it can talk!).

- **Create a personal website.** We discussed important elements to include in your website earlier. It is the top way to control the narrative built around your brand as a Strategic Business Influencer. A personal website carries the most weight around your name when it comes to where AI pulls information from and traditional search engine optimization.

- **Keep your online presence updated.** If your websites, social media profiles, or old blogs have dated information or are still live, even if they are not coming up on page 1 of Google, AI will pull this information to respond to prompts about you. It is more important than ever that you spend time understanding where you have a presence online and controlling as much information as you can by keeping your profiles up-to-date. This is why conducting the executive online brand audit is crucial to do every year with your brand.

- **Consistently feed AI fresh content.** Your online presence as a Strategic Business Influencer is not a set-it-and-forget-it strategy. In fact, this approach will only cause harm in the long run. Look for opportunities to feed AI fresh content through social media posts, blogs, or PR opportunities like interviews, podcasts, articles, and so on. Press opportunities hold a lot of weight because their websites have a higher volume of traffic. Increasing this activity is also a great way to outrank old press you cannot control over time. In part 2, I'll walk through how to balance the necessity of managing your online content without it interfering with your day job.

With user intent being the driver of AI, search will become even more personalized and humanized. This is good news for you if you are focusing your attention on delivering value online as a Strategic Business

Influencer. Having a strategy focused on educational intent is what will stand out in an AI-driven world.

PROTECTING YOUR BRAND STARTS NOW

I'll never forget meeting one CEO in Montreal. We were both attending a leadership conference and, during a coffee break, she mentioned something that stopped me in my tracks: Her brand's first impression was actively harming her company. Now, this wasn't your typical branding issue—this was the result of a conscious decision she had made to distance herself from any association with her personal brand. She thought removing herself from the narrative would fix the issue. Instead, it had the opposite effect. It blocked her from key business development opportunities.

Curious, I sat down with her after the session to dig deeper. We pulled up a private browser, and right there, the second result under her LinkedIn profile hit like a gut punch—her personal website URL, but with a description that could only be described as horrific. Clicking the link, we were taken to a scathing Glassdoor review written by a former disgruntled employee and riddled with damaging accusations.

It turns out she had never purchased her own name's URL. The disgruntled employee had. It was a digital nightmare. Her entire reputation was hijacked by someone with a vendetta. As a leader, you know there can be unfortunate people who do not become a fit for your organization and you have to make the difficult decision to part ways. The fallout from this was huge—business partners began to hesitate, potential deals fell through, and the trust she had worked so hard to build was unraveling.

What made it worse?

The solution wasn't a quick fix. To reclaim her identity, this CEO had to embark on a full personal rebranding journey, even incorporating her middle name to distance herself from the damage. Building a new presence took time, requiring consistency, diligence, and a careful strategy to stay aligned with her new identity.

It's a reminder that in today's digital age, if you don't own your personal brand, someone else will—and the consequences can be disastrous.

I say all of this not to scare you but to reinforce that being intentional and aware of your first impression is not ego-driven. It's setting you up for accelerated success and protecting you from harmful brand repercussions if you do not take ownership of your brand online. Online brands matter to everyone, but the moment you choose to be an entrepreneur or leader is when your online impression becomes vitally important. The best thing you can do in your role as the leader of the company is to take the time to create an impression that will represent your company proudly.

If you are just starting your company, do not wait to do this right. Getting this right from the beginning will allow you to "earn" a lot of impressions you would otherwise have to pay for if you were leading with your corporate brand. You can always enhance your impression with new opportunities and milestones. If you are a seasoned leader who needs some image CPR, start with reevaluating your current image and focus first on the assets you can control. You will be surprised at the difference it can make with just a few of the right tweaks. I learned that so many entrepreneurs started their businesses seeking to have full control and own their destiny and success. Why would you not treat your brand the same way?

Step 3

BUILD A FOUNDATION FOR AUDIENCE OWNERSHIP

It was 2021 at the EY Strategic Growth Forum when I met Sarah Dusek, an award-winning entrepreneur whose presence was magnetic even in a room full of industry giants. She had been named one of Ernst & Young's EY Entrepreneurial Winning Women, an honor that represented her incredible journey. In 2018, she sold her business, Under Canvas, for a staggering $100 million. With that milestone achieved, Sarah was ready to start new ventures, and you could see the excitement in her eyes as she shared her plans.

Sarah had a big vision of what she wanted to do next. Her goal as a Strategic Business Influencer was to build a platform that would allow her to demystify the funding process for women and advocate for ventures that not only turned a profit but also made a real impact in the world. As she shared her vision, I couldn't help but feel inspired by her experience, purpose, and determination.

One of the companies she cofounded that she was particularly excited about was Engyma Ventures, an investment fund aimed at empowering women entrepreneurs in Sub-Saharan Africa. Sarah had discovered that women-led businesses in that region were woefully underfunded, and she was determined to change that. She was raising her first fund and had already crafted an application process designed to attract a pipeline of companies—businesses that she and her partners could vet and ultimately invest in.

Sarah utilized her brand as an established entrepreneur to build visibility for Engyma Ventures and the investment opportunities available for women entrepreneurs in Sub-Saharan Africa. She crafted a strategy that would not only raise awareness among investors but also build an email list of potential portfolio companies that fit Engyma's investment profile. These businesses needed to be founded or led by women, scalable, and, most importantly, they had to demonstrate a unique and defensible business proposition with a clear purpose and proven growth potential.

Bringing her vision to life, she launched a highly targeted campaign. Every press effort, social media post, and email she sent to the list of over 4,000 subscribers she had built up was designed to lead the right entrepreneurs to the Engyma Ventures website. Potential applicants were driven to an eligibility quiz on the website to self-qualify and be considered for the fund. The email list she leveraged might not sound like much by today's vanity metrics, but this list was highly valuable to the fund. When the first open application period rolled around, Sarah's team had a record-setting number of applicants. Her visibility drove interest from quality, prequalified women-led businesses that would fuel Engyma Ventures' future growth and mission.

Engyma Ventures was just the beginning. Sarah continued to expand her influence, launching Few and Far, an eco-travel company that enabled guests to experience the great outdoors while contributing to environmental conservation. She even penned a bestselling book, *Thinking Bigger*, to educate women on how to fund and scale their businesses.

What struck me most about Sarah's journey was that she was not caught up in having millions or even hundreds of thousands of followers, although those will come for her with time. What she focused her time on was far more valuable—strategically building an audience of entrepreneurs and investors who were deeply aligned with her mission. Sarah had mastered the art of being a Strategic Business Influencer. Every venture, every initiative, was a natural extension of the brand she had built, rooted in trust, purpose, and impactful connections. And her brand gave each of those new ventures a jump start that would not have been possible without it. And as I watch her continued success, it is affirmed that this is the key to sustainable influence in today's world. You don't need millions of followers to make millions in impact. You just need the right ones.

Most entrepreneurs come to me with one burning question: "How do I grow my following and go viral?" They're eager for that social media explosion, convinced that if they could just crack the code, their business would skyrocket overnight. Maybe you have felt like you were spinning your wheels with your time or investment into social media or PR because you were not seeing any business results. It's understandable—social media has convinced businesses that building a massive audience quickly is the key to all success. But here's the kicker: While chasing virality might sound tempting, it's not where the real power lies in today's digital landscape. You have to have the right data acquisition strategy alongside a strong marketing strategy to see sustained success long term. A strong data acquisition strategy will keep your business from being a one-hit wonder.

At the end of the day, we must remember that social media platforms are businesses too. If you find a paid strategy that works well on Instagram, over time, it is in Instagram's best interests to shift its algorithm and find ways for you to feed them more dollars. Direct relationships are far more powerful than allowing third parties to own the connection to your audience.

Our agency has worked with a well-known global brand for over 15 years. Back in 2013, we had grown their Facebook following from only 2,000 likes to more than a million. We saw this brand thrive on Facebook because the platform's audience aligned perfectly with its target audience of middle-aged women. They were getting insane levels of engagement on posts and increasing revenue with the product campaigns that were being featured on their page. We thought a Facebook strategy was the golden ticket to growth for this brand. But then on a dark day that some of you in marketing might remember, Facebook completely changed its algorithm overnight in 2013. This algorithm shift made it much harder for businesses to have their content organically seen by users. Facebook was no longer going to show the brand's content to followers just because they liked the page—they started gatekeeping business page content from users' main Facebook feed unless businesses were paying to be seen. Their goal was to push businesses into utilizing the Facebook advertising feature so they would pay to get access to those following their page moving forward. That shift for Facebook was successful in skyrocketing their advertising revenue, making up as much as 97% of Meta's revenue in recent years.[1] The same shift toward a pay-to-play model was soon repeated on all social platforms. This made our team—and marketers around the world—face a harsh reality: Brands do not own the audiences built on these social media or search platforms. We are merely accessing an audience that platforms own at the end of the day. This is why your mindset as a business owner around the long-term goal of your marketing efforts might need to change—you don't want to build an audience on real estate someone else owns; you want to reach that audience and lead them back to real estate *you* own.

Another challenge to relying heavily on digital advertising to grow your audience is the shift in privacy regulations. Over the past several years, we have seen consumer data become less accessible through third-party applications like traditional advertising mediums, Google, Facebook, Instagram, and LinkedIn. Some of you might remember what I call the golden days of Facebook advertising, when you could pinpoint clearly where your dollars were being spent, down to job title, interests, other pages liked, and zip code. When it came to lead gener-ation and advertising, you could almost guarantee the number of leads you would receive and tailored quality. The days of brands being able to hyper-target consumers and generate targeted revenue solely on Face-book or Google advertising are gone. Much of this is due to giants like Apple and Meta being held rightfully accountable for the unethical col-lection and utilization of data without a user's full knowledge or consent. These conversations have led to the launch of Apple's opt-in feature now requiring third-party developers to ask permission to track users' data. With only 44% of US iPhone users opting in, this new feature has chal-lenged brands, resulting in more expensive advertising campaigns, and hindered the ability to run accurate retargeting campaigns.[2] As these conversations surface, I imagine we will see more restrictions across North America and European countries on third-party use of customer data. Building a customer acquisition strategy around paid media alone is costly and not sustainable because you have to continuously feed the algorithms to get you there. This has forced many businesses to cast a wider net or deploy more dollars to test campaigns with every target and algorithm shift these platforms roll out. This makes it extremely difficult for small to mid-sized businesses to keep up because we do not have those dollars to waste. What results is an unfair fight where smaller companies often lose, which is one of the reasons I am so passionate about the focus of this book. I see similar emerging social media ad platforms go through the same cycle, and businesses get caught up in deploying all their dollars for that viral moment and exposure, but when they get that opportunity, they leave the power up to the platform they do not own. In today's media environment, owning your data is no longer a luxury—it's a necessity.

But it's not just privacy changes that are making waves. Research shows that consumers, particularly post-pandemic, are becoming increasingly protective of their personal information. According to the 2022 Digital Consumer Trends Index, people are still willing to share their data—but with higher expectations than ever. They want personalized experiences, and they demand that brands use their data responsibly.

For entrepreneurs and brand leaders, this is a major shift. No longer can you rely on the quick-fix wins provided by third-party platforms that carry your message to a targeted, curated audience. Instead, you need to own the connection to your audience. This means rethinking how you acquire and manage data, focusing on first-party data and delivering real, personalized value. It's time to build a direct relationship with your audience that's rooted in trust. After all, when you control your data—and the connection to your audience—you control your future. So, if your strategy is currently leaning on social media ads or PR campaigns without focusing on data ownership, it's time to hit pause and reevaluate.

The question you should be asking isn't how you can get the most out of social media ads; it's how you can start owning your audience. The answer? Start by creating owned media assets—like your website, blog, or email list—that you control. When the third-party platforms fall short, your owned data will keep your business thriving. Trusting a third party to mediate your valuable relationships is too risky; you want permission to communicate directly with your audience how you want and when you want.

WHERE YOU HAVE OWNERSHIP
AND WHERE YOU DO NOT

So, what platforms can you utilize to build an audience you own?

In today's environment, three categories of media should be

integrated to provide different levels of control and reach for Strategic Business Influencers: rented, earned, and owned media. If you have a background in marketing, these three categories are most likely familiar and are definitely not new, but they are important to understand in the context of brand ownership.

The definition of *rented media* is a platform on which you control the content that goes out, but you do not own the relationship with the audience; the platform does. Advertising is a more obvious activity that is in the rented media category. When submitting an ad to a publication, you provide the ad copy and graphic design, but it goes out to a publication that owns the connection and relationship to the audience. Therefore, you are renting that audience exposure. The same circumstances apply when it comes to your social media channels as I mentioned in the 2013 Facebook example earlier in this chapter. You are renting visibility to your followers because you do not own your connection with them; the platform does. Think about it like gathering an audience on real estate someone else owns—it can be valuable but the owner has the final say on your ability to reach that audience.

The next category of media is *earned media*, which involves being invited onto someone else's platform to deliver your message, ultimately giving your audience the impression that you have earned your way there. Earned media can include your awards, media coverage, referrals, books, and speaking opportunities. This category can do a lot for building your credibility and visibility, along with trust, which is why I have dedicated the next chapter to it, but you have little to no control over how or when your message goes out.

Our last category is *owned media*, and in this chapter, we will spend most of our time dissecting how to reach and build an audience in this category. The definition of owned media is all the assets where you fully own the relationship to your audience. Your goal as a Strategic Business Influencer is to utilize the exposure you receive in rented media and earned media to grow your owned media audience. This category is where you can master control of data that rivals large institutions when done strategically. Owned media assets include your websites, email list, text or phone subscription list, physical addresses, a podcast (if produced independently), or any proprietary software.

This is where you might be reading this and thinking, *Did I pick up a marketing book from 2015?*

Yes, some of these formats might feel a bit archaic, but at the end of the day, data in these formats are what you need to be focused on growing for the long term. Not all formats might make sense for your business—for example, a physical mailing address might not be needed if you will never do any direct mail marketing. Your goal, though, should be to accumulate as many data points as possible from any qualified lead that comes across your brand. Having your audience follow you on your LinkedIn channel is no longer enough. Your follower count means nothing if you don't have control over how your brand is able to interact with your audience long-term regardless of what LinkedIn may decide to do with their algorithm.

Now, I share all this caution against relying too heavily on social media fully knowing I dedicated an entire chapter on how to drive leads with the right social media strategy later in this book. So I want to be clear: I'm not saying social media is the enemy, and you should stay completely clear of it. My goal is to help you shift your mindset to a bigger-picture marketing goal of building an audience you can have ownership of long-term. Your goal should be to attract the right visibility on these platforms and then drive them back with a value-driven prompt that encourages a prospect to take action on an asset that you own.

I also want to encourage serial entrepreneurs reading this book to think beyond just your business's owned assets. I sat down for a beer at Suds Monkey, one of my favorite breweries in Austin, Texas, with an entrepreneur who had exited his business the year prior. After riding

the high of his successful exit, as he should have, he, like most entrepreneurs, was ready to begin the next venture. He was launching a
new service to the same target market and industry as his previous
company. It was not going to be competitive with his prior product line
but an entirely new service to forward his mission of healthy, whole living. Throughout our conversation, it became clear that every asset and
piece of audience leverage he'd carefully built over the past decade had
been sold off with his previous company, leaving him without the foundation he'd hoped to use for launching this new service. He had also
been a leader completely behind the scenes and had no name recognition in the space outside of his past company's brand name. This presented his new service with several challenges, and throughout a couple
of beers, we had to face the grim reality that he had to start this new
venture completely from scratch. It was almost like his hard-earned
work in this industry he'd dedicated himself to over the past 10 years
never happened. Ultimately, he decided to start his marketing efforts
for his new company with a smart data acquisition strategy. He crafted
a strategy to grow his email list and data points ahead of his service
launch as he started to build the right first impression online that tied
his brand to the proven success of his prior company online. Ultimately,
the launch of his new service was successful due to the type of leader
he was. The reality he had to face, though, was that success could have
been accelerated if he had built his thought leadership and looked for
opportunities to acquire audience data with an executive brand strategy alongside his company.

If you have just started your business, it is best to start your data
acquisition from the jump. But if you are like most business owners and
haven't paid careful attention to customer or prospect data, it is never
too late to start. I'd encourage you to look at your assets and determine
where to shift your audience to more ownership. Don't trust anyone
else with your audience. Build connections you can own access to at

any time, nurture them, and use social platforms as a tool, not the foundation.

EVALUATING YOUR AUDIENCE OWNERSHIP

As you consider this strategy mindset, I encourage you to evaluate your current audience's level of ownership. Do you have your audience weighted in the right areas where you have full ownership of your connection with them? Or are you at risk of going through gatekeepers consistently to access them? Taking 10 minutes to conduct this analysis can change your business's trajectory for the next 10 years. All you are doing with this evaluation is a simple numbers exercise.

Determine on a sheet of paper where you have connectivity or exposure with your audience. I want you to think through assets like your email list, website, social media channels, review platforms, press hits, text subscriptions list, physical addresses, events you attend, and brick-and-mortar locations if applicable. What is the size or level of exposure to your audience on each platform? As a reminder, it is okay if your audience sizes are not big—most are not. It is the right followers that matter. At this point, you are purely estimating and writing down audience size per platform.

While you are working on listing out your audiences, be sure to add exposure to not only your business, but also your personal platforms. Add up your total audience exposure and start assigning percentages of audience weight to each platform you have written down. This will allow you to see where your audience exposure is weighted the most for your brand. If you are visual like me, creating a pie chart visual of these percentages will give you a clearer picture of your audience breakdown.

As you review your list, shade in on your pie chart the platforms you know you have full control over your audience connection. For example, on your website, you have full control over what users see and experience every time they go to your website link. You can control what is displayed on your website fully, from the text to the creative. You also control your communication with your email, text subscription, physical mailing lists, and brick-and-mortar locations. You might use different platforms to deploy these communications, but ultimately if you own this information and it's a form of contact, you can utilize it at any time and fully control the message going out.

Platforms you will leave unshaded might include your social media accounts because you have no control over their algorithm. Review platforms are not controlled if you have business reviews featured online because you cannot dictate what is seen on these platforms. You also have limited control over press hits, awards, or events. You do have the ability to give a good interview or submit information you want an article to include, but you cannot control what goes out on their platforms or when. This type of exposure is extremely valuable for your business.

Once you evaluate your owned assets, examine your pie chart. Is the majority of your chart shaded or unshaded? Where is your audience weighted the most?

If you are looking at a mostly unshaded pie chart, do not be discouraged. This is what I see when I do this exercise with most business owners. I encourage you to utilize this exercise to give you clarity on where to focus on growing your marketing efforts moving forward. If you're staring at a mostly unshaded pie chart, your goal moving forward is to create a strategy to siphon off the exposure from your unshaded areas and convert them to your own shaded assets. The growth of an audience you own takes time and starts with a clear, intentional strategy. If you can shift your mindset and long-term focus into growing these owned assets alongside your marketing initiatives, you will most likely begin to see lower customer acquisition costs, quicker sales cycles, and higher conversion rates.

SHIFTING TO A DATA OWNERSHIP MINDSET

There is limited, short-term value in hiring a marketing agency to come in and grow your social media audience if there is no conversion strategy to an owned media asset for you. If you only pour time and resources into growing assets you do not fully own, you are putting significant risk on your business. If you think of your audience as real estate assets, it's like you are throwing resources at rent versus building equity in ownership. Audiences on those platforms could disappear overnight, and you could do nothing about it. Do you remember what happened to your Myspace profile? Some of you who were part of the first wave of the social media generation reading this book might. You are an entrepreneur because you were born with an ownership mindset. Why would you not have the same fortitude when it comes to building your audience?

How to Acquire Ownership of Your Audience

As you analyze your shaded versus unshaded areas of your audience pie chart, you might realize that a conversion strategy is needed to grow your audience ownership. To have sustainable, long-term brand success, your goal should be to have most of your pie chart shaded. To accomplish this, you must determine a lead magnet offering to attract your audience from areas you do not control and convert them to assets you own, like your email list.

Investopedia describes a lead magnet as "a free item or service that is given away for the purpose of gathering contact details."[3] I see many leaders who spend thousands of dollars generating eyeballs and visibility through social media, advertising, and PR, only to be frustrated that their marketing strategy is not producing results for their business. It was only after I looked at their website that I realized there is no clear strategy to collect data and convert these audiences to assets where leaders can keep the conversation going with audience members who have shown an interest but are not ready to buy. The heyday of converting your audience solely through clickbait links and slick marketing funnels is gone because your audience sees right through them. These online funnels are focused on infomercial-styled selling, and consumers know that. There is no easy button for curating your most valuable online audience asset, your owned media list.

Your approach to converting your audience to assets you own should mirror how you interact with meeting potential prospects at an industry conference. For example, when you attend an industry conference and meet a connection that could be a referral source for your business, you leave that event with their information and find opportunities to continue the conversation outside the event to, ultimately, create a mutually beneficial relationship. Your goal is to use additional conversations to get to know them, learn more about how you can support them, and understand what would be rewarding to them in a referral partnership. These principles are Networking 101 basics that have worked for the past 100 years.

The basics of building your online-owned audience are applied Networking 101 principles at scale. You must find the right value proposition with your lead magnet to collect more information from those interested in your brand to continue a customized follow-up conversation, just like you would with in-person leads. Of course, there are circumstances where prospects are ready to buy after one conversation, but with most businesses, that is a rarity. If you count on having a one-interaction close, you might be leaving a high volume of opportunities on the table. Most high-touch business development processes will take several conversations and time to build trust before a customer is ready to buy or a strategic partner is ready to refer prospects.

As you brainstorm the best lead magnet to convert more of your audience to owned assets, I encourage you to think about those initial conversations you have after meeting a prospect in person. A good place to prompt your brainstorming is by thinking through the following questions.

- What is the immediate concern or issue they need to resolve?
- If their problem is solved tomorrow, how would they benefit personally?
- What is keeping them from being able to solve the problem on their own?
- Are there pieces of additional information I need to better understand how to support them?

These are most likely the questions on which they are seeking expertise from an experienced subject matter expert. Exploring these questions will allow you to reverse engineer what is most valuable to a prospect in the initial interaction moment to build a lead magnet around.

A successful lead magnet should always involve a mutual value exchange between you and your audience. It is not just about what information you can gather; rather, it is about the most valuable information you can give away. This is the mindset to master as a Strategic Business Influencer.

The type of lead magnet category you utilize to collect data is imperative. To get past your consumer's guard, the lead magnet must have a high perception of value for your acquisition rate to your owned audience assets to be successful. As you begin analyzing the best lead magnet for your business, I'll share four of the most common lead magnet categories we see utilized in today's environment and the average success each category has.

The Sign-Up Form

This is the lead magnet that you will most certainly see on every website you visit. It's the typical email, phone number, or address sign-up form where you can input your information to receive what is described most of the time as vague "news and updates" on a product or service. With how tightly consumers safeguard their information today, you can imagine why this lead magnet is typically the lowest converting in the landscape.

This type of lead magnet asks users to blindly trust you with their data. How often does blind trust convert in business? Almost never. Unless you have one of the most well-known brands in the world, this category of lead magnet will do nothing for you. You might be thinking, *Paige, this is the lead magnet I see on every website I visit. If it does not work, why do most people use it?* That is a fair question. Most of the time, this lead magnet is a standard data collection point that is included by the website development team and is an afterthought of the leader when they approve the website.

This category of lead magnet is often present when there is a fly-by-the-seat-of-your-pants approach to collecting data. Although we know data collection is important, there is a desire to delay a follow-up plan until data is collected or the plan is to sit on the data until it is needed. With this category, do not hold your breath that you will have the data to experience either problem because there is no clear perceived value for your audience, so your conversion, at best, is most likely 2%.[4] The rule of thumb with lead magnets is—if the value is not mutual or clear, it is not a good strategy.

As an exception to this rule, I do believe there is value in including a data collection sign-up form in the global footer of your website. This means that no matter the page you view on the website, there is a sign-up form at the bottom, most likely next to the website's copyright language. This allows a website user to opt in to continue the conversation as they read more of your content at any point in their website user experience journey. This lead magnet category should only be utilized in the global footer when another category of lead magnet serves as the main acquisition strategy through the interior pages of the website.

The Information Download

This category of lead magnet is what most often comes to mind for B2B businesses. An information download most commonly provides one of the following in exchange for customer data.

- Research study
- Free e-book
- White paper
- Workbook
- Free chapter

This acquisition strategy has a much higher conversion rate than the sign-up form because the exchange of value is clear and intentional. On average, studies show this lead magnet category converts at best 10% of website visitors.[5] Although this category can be successful with the right visibility, there are two challenges to look out for if you are considering the information download as your lead magnet.

1. You are taking an educated guess that the download you provide will give the prospect the right value to keep them engaged in your business development process before learning more about them.

2. If you are just starting to build your brand, there could be a barrier to trust. If this is the first time they are coming across your website, there may not be a strong enough perceived value to understand the actual value of the download.

The Discount Code

Because I am a bargain shopper at heart, I'm a sucker for this lead magnet category. Most will experience this lead magnet as a pop-up on a product website offering a 10% discount on your first purchase if you sign up for their email or text subscription list. To let you in on a secret, I have multiple junk email addresses I give them that I never check to access the discount. Yes, this is the level I embarrassingly admit I go to for the satisfaction of winning what a brand makes me think is a deal.

This category of lead magnet typically converts anywhere from 5% to 10% for most B2C and consumer packaged goods (CPG) brands.[6] The attraction of the discount code is that it's an easy strategy, and can have multiple benefits when utilized in the right industry. The discount code, when used strategically, can not only support ownership of customer data, it can also boost repeat transactions when utilized in customer campaigns. This is why we see events like Black Friday and Cyber Monday now become recognized national holidays. How many of you have held out on a purchase in anticipation of seeing what they discount the price of a product to?

The partial concern of this category is that it fulfills a brand's short-term needs but oftentimes does not provide the best customer behavior or lifetime value. Starting an interaction with a steep discount code can lead to cycles of unpredictability in customer behavior, lower perceived value, and lower margins if not presented strategically. Not all discount codes are bad, but there must be a clear look at how it will impact margins and customer perception.

If you are in a B2B space, I want to caution against using a discount code. Save any discount conversations for your contract negotiations. Do not advertise any discount or free service publicly unless you want to be stuck in a vicious cycle of never growing your price beyond your advertised value. You do not have to discount your prices to increase your customer data acquisition rate. If you are a CPG brand, I would encourage you to look at integrating an added-value code into your strategy that could potentially boost your brand's perceived value over time. A Texas grooming product company, Supply, has executed this strategy well. They leaned into an added-value code strategy by offering a select number of free blades after joining their email list and purchasing a full-priced razor. This incentive brings them into a full-price purchase that will ultimately upsell a customer into a subscription purchase, increasing their customer's lifetime value.

The Self-Discovery Assessment

This category of lead magnet continues to drive success and value for brands across several industries at high converting rates, often more than double the other categories. Why? It's less about the brand and more about your audience. It's powerful when you can create an experience that gives a prospect not only instant gratification but also high-perceived knowledge about themselves. Humans are naturally curious to learn more about themselves and addicted to self-discovery.[7] It is what is at the core of our nature. An assessment provides a low barrier to entry opportunity for a prospect to experience the value you can generate in a way that speaks directly to their core.

The approach to creating the right assessment for your brand can depend on the target audience you are pursuing and your Influence ID. Two types of assessments should be considered as you analyze the right approach.

1. **A measured assessment.** This type of assessment provides a ranking, score, or percentage a prospect can improve over time. The results should be accompanied by action steps on what a prospect should do to enhance their score in the future.
2. **An identification assessment.** This type of assessment places a prospect in an archetype or category that uncovers key characteristics or behavior. The results of the identification assessment should guide clear objectives on how this knowledge can be applied to improve performance or daily life. Their

result will most likely be the same no matter how often they take the assessment.

A self-discovery assessment is one of the most powerful tools you can create for your business. In addition to the prospect experience being the reason it performs at a high conversion rate, it also provides tangible, top-of-the-funnel data points about each prospect coming into contact with your brand based on how they answer each question. With this strategy, you are not only converting your audience to owned assets by having them fill out their information to complete the assessment, but you are also able to gather audience data and segment it in various ways. As we established earlier, data is power. The more you can learn about your audience on the front end, the more targeted your business development process can be. This could lead to shorter lead cycles and higher close rates for your business.

As you begin working on creating a self-discovery assessment for your business, I encourage you to avoid a few common traps that will leave you spinning your wheels. Our team has learned what works (and what doesn't) by building assessments that have been taken over a million times. If you want your assessment to drive results, avoid the following pitfalls.

- An assessment with all questions and no robust result segments is not an assessment; it is, at best, a form or survey. It will not convert.
- Simplicity always wins. There is a time and place for complex assessments, but they do not work as lead magnets. If you have a great idea for a complex assessment, you can always build an additional paid assessment offering.
- Keep it focused on evaluating the quiz taker, not a group. There

is more engagement when the focus stays on the individual quiz taker.

- There are no rules for the perfect amount of questions to include in an assessment. As long as the assessment experience is value-driven and engaging, you will convert.
- A strong assessment is not a set-it-and-forget process. Assessments should be dynamic as your brand continues to evolve. Do not be afraid to run A/B tests with your audience to learn what works.

If an assessment is the right strategy for you, there are a few platforms I recommend to help you develop a final product for your website.

- Catch Engine, catchengine.com. I might be biased on this recommendation—it is the system our firm has utilized for several years for custom development.
- Typeform, typeform.com.
- Outgrow, outgrow.co.

While producing and maintaining a self-discovery assessment requires a lot of work on the front end, you can unlock a level of sophistication in your marketing strategy that allows you to maximize the hyper-targeted value you can deliver to prospects, a tool that was only once reserved for advertising platform giants.

DRIVING YOUR AUDIENCE'S ATTENTION TO YOUR LEAD MAGNETS

As you review your audience pie chart, look at the areas that are not shaded. These unshaded assets you do not own are where your lead magnet needs to be plugged consistently in content, not your product or service. Audiences will be turned off by the overly promotional sales push. This is where your value-driven lead magnet as a Strategic Business Influencer will come into play.

Your goal with each unshaded area is to prompt those audiences with content to take action by walking away from that platform and landing on your website lead magnet experience, allowing you to capture their information in the process. The link to the lead magnet on your website is where you should consistently send your social media followers, podcast listeners, article readers, and presentation audiences. In your call-to-action language, drive home the value of the resource for your audience. The more value-driven, the more successful your audience acquisition will be.

CEO and founder Lisa Sun is a master at capturing and converting her audience. As the founder and CEO of Gravitas, a clothing company that promotes body positivity and self-confidence, Lisa became a sought-after speaker and built her brand as a Strategic Business Influencer. In 2023, she was gearing up to launch her first bestselling book, *Gravitas: The 8 Strengths That Redefine Confidence.* Her calendar for the upcoming year was filled with events where she would share her keynote. There was extensive time and relentless work from Lisa and her team to get her message in front of the women she could impact. Lisa knew it was vital to maximize and leverage every opportunity to grow her audience. Instead of relying solely on her book to grow her audience, she created an assessment that audience members could take for free to discover their confidence language. At every stage she stepped on that year, she shared the link to the assessment with that audience as a free resource for women. Within a year of her book launch, she organically grew her email list with the call-to-action to her lead magnet assessment to over 20,000 women. Lisa's book is now a *USA Today* bestseller and has been translated into other languages, allowing her to widen her impact helping women find their gravitas.

NURTURING A RELATIONSHIP WITH
AN AUDIENCE YOU OWN

Once you establish your lead magnet and start steering your audience toward a clear call-to-action, collecting data is only the starting point. What you do with your prospect data once it is collected is just as important as obtaining it. To ease your data collection process, integrate a customer relationship management (CRM) management tool with the back end of your brand website. Most tools are free or require only a low monthly cost. Most tools on the market get the job done unless you are in need of complex integrations. The important things you are looking for in a CRM are automatic data integration with your website lead magnet, the ability to segment data into lists, and tools to draft and send out communication via email, text, or physical mail.

The ability to segment your data is crucial. If you are dumping all of your prospect data into one list in your CRM and blasting communication, you are throwing content out there like darts at a wall. You will get the most out of your data if it is segmented at the point of collection. Segmenting will give you an understanding of where a lead is coming from and how to best continue the conversation with them. Back to Networking 101, you want it to mirror in-person discovery conversations by picking up the communication where you last left off.

To create clear segmentation, you must decide what data is needed to qualify a lead when creating your lead magnet. For some businesses, this could be a geotargeted zip code, job title, employee count, revenue size, age, or industry. Pick one or two data points that matter the most for your ideal client profile when it comes to demographic collection. Requiring too many demographic data points can turn off your prospects and lower your conversion rate.[8] One strategy to collect more data points while providing value to your audience is embedding a few discovery questions into an assessment lead magnet. The way an assessment taker answers these questions can determine if they are an ideal profile client fit and even unveil pain points you can follow up on. In your CRM, create clarity and label how each list is organized based on the data points you determined matter most for your brand. This will set you up for long-term success as you continue nurturing relationships with prospects and customers.

Unfortunately, I have a lot of leaders I speak with who have email or text subscription lists built and segmented, but they cannot recall the last time they sent communication out to their lists, if ever. This delayed approach can do more harm than good for your brand and often happens when a nurture strategy is not in place. When someone hands you their data, it signals they are knocking on your door and ready for the first step into your sales funnel. If they knock on that door and no one answers for three months, the likelihood of them still being on your doorstep when you decide it is finally time to open it and communicate with them is low. Most audience members will be turned off by this approach, and it can have a damaging effect on your brand's reputation. They will sense you are only reaching out to sell them something versus deliver value.

Once a prospect is added to your owned audience asset, like an email list, the first flow of communication they should receive is what is called a drip sequence campaign. This is a series of prewritten messages that are sent to them over a period of time, typically four to five points of communication over several weeks. It is best to create a few different drip sequences directed at your top-segmented audience lists for a customized prospect experience. This might feel overwhelming at the moment, but once the messages are created, you can set up your CRM on a schedule to send the messages automatically once their information is added to a segmented list. The time you put into creating and setting up value-driven drip sequences on the front end can accelerate trust with your prospects and encourage them to take the next step in your sales funnel.

Once a prospect goes through an introductory drip sequence, you must continue to nurture the relationship the same way you would after a few in-person interactions with a qualified prospect. Ongoing nurturing should be on a regular cadence that is typically monthly or quarterly for most brands. You want to strike a fine balance between nurturing your audience without overwhelming them. More important than frequency is the content of your communication. The more value you can give away to your audience, the quicker you can build trust and long-term loyalty. Strategic business influencers prioritize driving education and entertainment with their content over pushing a product or service. This means there is no magic number to frequency when the content is valuable and consistent.

As you shift your strategy toward audience ownership, keep an eye on where your audience is weighted as your brand grows. Trusting too many third parties to mediate valuable relationships that are core to your business is too risky. I get that some of the information in these first three steps might feel incredibly tactical, but you must look inward first to get your foundation right. My hope is that these exercises allow you to examine if you are reflecting the trust, credibility, and differentiation your company needs. Taking the time to renew your Influence ID, evaluate your first impression, and set up your platform for audience ownership will allow you to produce results with the following steps to win over your customers with PR, content marketing, and driving referrals.

PART 2

PART 2

Step 4

CREATE PR BUZZ FROM YOUR SMARTPHONE

Imagine this scenario: It's the night before your big investor presentation, and you are busy reviewing your slides and talking points. You're ready to own the room and build trust through a measured presentation of your market positioning, product fit, and vision for the future. But while you are preparing to make a great first impression in the boardroom, the investor you're going to be meeting with is sitting on her couch googling your name in preparation for the meeting. The first impression she gets tonight will cement your image in her mind before you even walk into her office. Google might make her inclined to trust you, or it might make her question why she even agreed to this meeting. Fortunately, her search results are working in your favor. She finds that guest column you wrote for Forbes.com and the article in *Harvard Business Review* that quoted you as an expert. Then she skims through quite a few hits from niche websites that cover your industry and others that cover your local business community. She also clicks on that podcast interview you did earlier in the year and spends 15 minutes learning more about your upbringing and the light bulb moment for your start-up. When the investor shuts her laptop, she's prepared to begin your pitch meeting with a favorable impression and a foundation of trust, giving you the benefit of the doubt.

That's the real power of PR in today's world—not people consuming a given media hit when it first runs, but digital results that act as word-of-mouth that can last forever. By strategically leveraging your PR and thought leadership, you can steadily build your credibility over time, as well as your clout as a Strategic Business Influencer.

This might sound surprising given my job, but I believe most entrepreneurs and leaders do *not* need full-blown corporate public relations to achieve their goals, at least in the short term. You don't have to break the bank by hiring a high-retainer PR firm, which is great news for bootstrapping small businesses. I have more good news for you: Quality PR is more accessible than ever before—once you learn how to apply a targeted, do-it-yourself approach.

As you scale your company, two crucial elements can make or break your success: credibility and trust. Whether you are setting up meetings with investors, pitching vendors, or trying to land that next-level client, it's hard to prove yourself without the validation of third-party media that your stakeholders already know and trust.

Both name-brand national media and niche media are powerful ways to gain exposure for your thought leadership. Each has its own benefits that can help you reach your goals, in different ways. Before we get into some examples, let's break down the differences and how Strategic Business Influencers should think about them.

THE AGE OF MICROMEDIA

When most leaders think about PR, they tend to envision being featured on mainstream media outlets like CNBC, the *Wall Street Journal*, or *Good Morning America*, as those were traditionally the platforms that provided visibility and credibility. These outlets held a high level of trust with their audiences, making a feature or appearance extremely impactful for a brand or business. But the way people consume media—and which media they trust—has evolved significantly over the past decade. In today's environment, people are consuming more media than ever before, but the majority of it falls under a new category called *micromedia*. Think podcasts, trade publications, and YouTube channels. These platforms may have relatively small audiences, but they have the power to connect niche audiences with specific industry experts, enabling a more targeted and trustworthy exchange of information.

Think of it this way: Would you rather have your message heard by 5,000 people who care about it, or 500,000 who don't?

Or think about it as a consumer of content rather than a producer. My commute to my office in Austin is about 30 to 40 minutes each way, depending on the traffic. To make the most of my time in the car every morning, I listened to my favorite radio show I mentioned in step 1, *The Bobby Bones Show*. It's a country music and talk show that started in Austin and has since moved its home base to Nashville, where it has scaled to nationwide syndication.

What captivated me the most about this show was its unique approach to interviews. While other hosts focused solely on interviewing big country music stars, Bobby Bones often brought in the songwriters and managers who work behind the scenes in the music industry. This not only provided me with fresh perspectives but also allowed me to gain valuable insights from those who played a pivotal role in shaping country music.

However, I soon realized that I only got a 5- to 7-minute segment with a songwriter or insider during my entire 30- to 40-minute commute. So, I started switching from the radio show to *Bobbycast*, which Bobby records as a separate podcast. He uses the podcast to air much longer interviews with the guests in his studio, about 30 minutes each. This means I get much more in-depth content about all those behind-the-scenes folks in the industry.

So, which is more valuable for a Bobby Bones guest—a short interview heard by a huge national audience or a longer, in-depth interview heard by a smaller but more passionate and loyal audience?

I've now started to make the same shift with all other subjects I want to stay up-to-date on, or entertained by, including marketing and leadership. I began to embrace the power of smaller, more targeted formats, including podcasts, newsletters, blogs, YouTube channels, and X (formerly Twitter) feeds. These micromedia outlets allow me to be more selective in how I invest my time and what I gain from each outlet.

This trend opens a wide array of opportunities for business leaders to demonstrate their credibility and expertise with the *right* audiences that match their goals. This is where trusted thought leadership comes into play. By consistently sharing valuable insights and expertise through micromedia channels, you can establish yourself as a go-to expert in your industry.

HOW TO PURSUE MICROMEDIA

PR and marketing gurus Barbara Cave Henricks and Rusty Shelton defined micromedia as access to "high-quality, niche information" in their book, *Mastering the New Media Landscape*.[1] The key to that description is "high-quality." People who are passionate about a subject are not going to stick around for mediocre media content.

Another huge challenge to building your PR strategy around micromedia is the sheer scale of possible outlets and formats. Just starting to research your field can be overwhelming! For instance, according to Listen Notes, there are now more than *three million* active podcasts.[2] With such a vast array of options, and the modest listenership associated with micromedia, you might wonder if it's even worth the effort.

The answer lies in the ability of targeted micromedia to drive results for a variety of goals, starting with industry-specific credibility. In industries like healthcare or tech, where credibility among peers is critical, landing coverage in trade publications such as TechCrunch or KevinMD can be vital for driving results. Those kinds of websites, podcasts, and influencer feeds can play a crucial role in targeted lead generation. By identifying and focusing on outlets that directly speak to your niche, you can leverage micromedia to drive a surprising quantity and quality of leads. And they can not only establish your business as trustworthy for customers, but can also win visibility with the potential influencers, investors, and partners you need.

Many leaders overlook micromedia opportunities, dismissing them because the audience numbers don't seem large enough to warrant their time and effort. But I encourage you to delve deeper into the descriptions of the audiences consuming various micromedia outlets. It is the *demographics and characteristics* of each outlet—not the total numbers—that hold the key to determining if an opportunity is worth your time.

Throughout my career, I have witnessed the power of micromedia get stronger and stronger. And I've seen some incredible results when my firm deploys a micromedia-driven PR strategy. For instance, let's see how this kind of campaign played out for a Zilker client called S3 Surface Solutions.

How Do You Get PR for a Subflooring Manufacturer?

In 2016, entrepreneur Jack Aspenson embarked on a mission to revolutionize construction manufacturing with his start-up, S3 Surface Solutions.

S3's niche is manufacturing concrete preparation, moisture barrier solutions, and adhesives for concrete subfloors. While this doesn't sound like the sexiest business, and while Cumming, Georgia, is not exactly Silicon Valley, S3 quickly surpassed eight figures in revenues while impressing its early customers with its innovative, sustainable, cost-saving solutions:

When I got the idea to start S3, I was actually working for another company that did commercial building restorations. While I was working there, I helped them build a new business to complement the restoration side of the business, which was an epoxy line. These historic commercial buildings were experiencing massive flooring failures, so I went out and found manufacturers to make unique epoxies that would help them. I realized through this process that the flooring market was a huge opportunity because there was not a lot of institutional knowledge of why their floors were failing. The market did not understand the physics and the chemistry behind how to fix certain problems like moisture mitigation to limit its effect on flooring. And I was sitting there with a product I knew could immediately lock down moisture.

Through market research, I found that competitors did not want to fix the problem. They wanted to put a Band-Aid on it because if you fixed it, you did not get recurring revenue. I wanted to challenge this industry norm and present the flooring industry with a permanent solution. This led us to engage with a few of the large flooring mills, and one of them took it and just ran with it. We then developed a very strong technical team and were able to put together what I consider an epiphany moment for the company—we came out with the S3 Surfaces Universal Sub Floor Systems. This was a never-before-seen industry approach, so there was a lot of education that had to go into what a systems approach meant.

S3 was created because I saw a problem. I saw a market and a competitive landscape that was not addressing the problem; instead, they were ignoring it. The sad thing was these challenges impacted at least 20% of the market. I was not trying to compete on a price point or feature benefit.

I believe that with most products, like adhesives, in the flooring indus-try, it is a race to the bottom price. All you are doing is buying customers by sacrificing margin. I didn't want to take that approach. I wanted to go after that 20% of the market where they really needed a solution to fix the ongoing problem. Having the lowest price was less of a concern for me. Quality and environmentally friendly solutions were my top concern so I developed the products around that. And that's how the S3 system came to be.[3]

Despite that fast start to S3, Jack faced a challenge: His ground-breaking products remained hidden from most of the industry. He and I discussed ways to bring visibility to his brand and ramp up lead gener-ation with architects, structural engineers, property managers, develop-ers, and end users. I was immediately impressed by S3's advancements in flooring technology, which made their products a dream come true for subcontractors and architects. We just needed to get the word out to the right audiences, and potential growth could be enormous.

Jack had a rare gift for simplifying complex science and conveying excitement about S3's offerings, which made him the best possible voice for representing their brand message. The question was how to use his voice in cost-effective ways.

The construction industry, as a whole, lagged behind most fields in adopting modern marketing tactics. Most companies featured mundane websites, boring trade show booths, text-heavy technical sheets, and old-looking Facebook pages with minimal content. If S3 wanted to differ-entiate itself, it needed a marketing strategy that was just as innovative as its products. Jack agreed, and together we developed three key initiatives to set S3 apart.

Elevating visual assets. We designed a new company style guide that projected innovation via meaningful colors and sleek typography. S3's visual strategy went beyond industry norms, extending to product labels, investor pitch presentations, an all-new website, and downloadable product information sheets. The new look turned heads because it was a far cry from the competition, which used extremely basic primary colors and block lettering.

Targeting micromedia. We helped S3 launch a targeted public relations campaign aimed at industry decision-makers. Instead of sending out traditional press releases or pitches, we crafted timely articles addressing industry pain points and evergreen educational content. And we focused on landing niche media that would be receptive to Jack's thought leadership, rather than wasting our time on more mainstream outlets that would surely have dismissed our outreach.

Within just eight months, S3 was featured in several industry-focused publications and podcasts, and Jack was building a reputation as an innovator, a flooring expert, and a rising star entrepreneur. Among the many media outlets that covered S3's story:

- *Floor Covering Installer*, a trade magazine with 38,000 subscribers. Its audience includes key decision-makers who buy in bulk: flooring installers, installation managers, contractors, and distributors for both residential and commercial construction.
- *Construction Executive*, a website with 63,000 unique visitors per month plus more than 12,000 newsletter subscribers. It's the flagship outlet for the Associated Builders and Contractors (ABC), a trade association for 21,000 member companies, including the nation's biggest contractors. A whopping 88% of *Construction Executive* subscribers are company owners or senior management.
- *Wood Floor Business*, which reaches 12,000 unique monthly visitors who are mostly flooring contractors, installers, and

builders. WFB publishes an annual guide to products and services in their industry. When it featured one of S3's new products, the coverage drove more traffic and downloads on the S3 website than the company had ever seen before.

- *Design News*, another influential trade publication. It featured Jack as a thought leader on supply chain agility—an issue that one of S3's new products was able to solve for customers.

Now let's be honest—are these media outlets as impressive as the *New York Times, 60 Minutes,* or *Good Morning America*? Of course not. Jack wouldn't be able to brag about them to strangers at cocktail parties. But that is actually the point: Strategic business influence isn't about bragging rights, vanity numbers, or fame; it is about accelerating trust with your stakeholders through effective marketing and authentic thought leadership. S3 gained more visibility, lead generation, and revenue growth from these highly targeted media opportunities than it could have by pursuing famous brand-name media. The construction and flooring communities respected S3's newly evident credibility, along with Jack's new reputation as a thought leader.

In fact, one of S3's most impactful media opportunities was the smallest in raw numbers, even smaller than the ones highlighted above. A podcast with just 1,500 monthly listeners interviewed Jack, and one of those 1,500 was the CEO of a major potential customer. The podcast led to an introduction, which led to one of S3's biggest breakthrough opportunities for new business development. Remember: *It's not the size, it's the audience.*

Remarketing of PR. Our third key initiative was to boost the initial impact and visibility of S3's media coverage by remarketing their PR hits. We featured and promoted the links on both the company's social media channels and Jack's personal platforms, especially on LinkedIn. This paid off because the coverage that showcased Jack's smart, thoughtful, and innovative approach popped up in search results whenever potential customers researched him and his company.

LinkedIn remarketing, in particular, became a wonderful driver of long-term growth. Although most architects were not using LinkedIn, the up-and-coming decision-makers who were most interested in innovation *were* active on the platform. Jack used LinkedIn to build new relationships with such architects and their firms, which paid off with more than 50 new, qualified leads in just a single quarter. Focusing on quality rather than quantity of leads worked even better than we had hoped.

By combining all these tactics, S3's campaign was nothing like a traditional new product launch or lead generation push. We focused on showing off the knowledge and expertise of S3's leaders, educating potential customers about their products, and demonstrating why S3 was an innovator in sustainability, cutting-edge technology, and decreasing project time.

While some CEOs would have resisted interviews with small outlets, Jack understood the value of becoming a Strategic Business Influencer. His focus on the right priorities propelled his company forward, breaking through the information clutter and differentiating S3 Surface Solutions from its competitors.

Like many Strategic Business Influencers, Jack has continued to boil the ocean with new innovations and ventures beyond his work at S3. He continues to build his brand tackling the cement industry, residential AI, building security, and speed of customer service with AI. Jack currently holds six patents across ventures and is on the road to garnering 30. Although he continues to add new spokes to his brand wheel, he shared with me that it all centers around his single brand mission—leaving a legacy of creating a safe and secure community.

WHAT ABOUT NAME-BRAND MEDIA?

Despite the clear benefits of micromedia, many business leaders are still drawn by the allure of major national media. They aspire to shine brightly in the kind of media spotlight their friends and family will recognize immediately, and they hire traditional PR firms to target such coverage.

Being featured in a major outlet can undoubtedly enhance your credibility and visibility. However, it's important to manage your expectations when it comes to the immediate impact on your business. While there are cases where a feature in a national outlet can directly result in a surge of new business and clients, that's actually the exception rather than the norm. Casting a wide net with name-brand media is more about establishing your presence and credibility within your industry.

You also need to manage your expectations around formats. Over the past decade, most magazines and newspapers have evolved beyond their traditional formats. Premium business publications such as the *Wall Street Journal, Harvard Business Review, Fortune, Forbes, Inc.,* and *Fast Company* all now have far more readers online than on paper and correspondingly larger reach and impact online. Some even reach several million monthly web visitors and e-newsletter subscribers. So, getting coverage in one of those formats can be a wonderful outcome, even if you can't show off a printed newspaper or magazine to your family.

Another caveat: With the vast amounts of content being generated by major outlets, your specific coverage can come and go in the blink of an eye. If you are fortunate enough to garner a feature in name-brand media, the true measure of success will be whether you strategically remarket it to maximize its impact. As soon as your coverage goes live, prominently display the media outlet's logo and link on your company and personal websites, ideally on the home pages. This ensures that when Google brings people to your page, they will immediately see a familiar and trusted logo, accelerating their perception of your credibility and trustworthiness.

You can also immediately start to include the outlet's name or logo in your pitch decks, on your social media platforms, and in any public-facing materials. Some may argue that this approach feels overly promotional, but doing it this way is actually less promotional than constantly talking about that time you were quoted in the *Wall Street Journal*. Once you have the right visual reminders in key locations, you won't have to explicitly mention it.

Another powerful way to make the most of name-brand media coverage is by arming your sales team with it. Encourage them to include a link to the coverage as part of every follow-up email they send to prospects. This strategy works even better when the featured article is a thought leadership piece that addresses a pain point affecting your ideal client or customer. By linking to coverage in a major outlet, your sales team will give customers supplementary value even before they close the sale. People appreciate this kind of information, and it can influence their ultimate decision to buy from your company.

Remember, the main goal when pitching name-brand media is boosting your credibility over the long run, not selling a few extra units the day or week the coverage runs. It's up to you to ensure that any hard-earned media gets seen by the right people through strategic remarketing.

THE HIDDEN VALUE OF AWARDS
FOR SMALL BUSINESS

Another credibility builder alongside name-brand media is award-driven PR. This category of PR can often be achieved quicker than name-brand media for small businesses. To be clear, I'm not talking about the pay-to-play, everyone wins an award common in some commodity-driven industries. Reputable awards have a nomination, extensive application, and judging process. Similar to media outlets, awards are also divided into two categories: name-brand recognition and category awards. Both categories can drive different results for your business. Name-brand awards are typically industry-agnostic awards at a national or global level. Awards like the Inc. 5000, Ernst & Young's Entrepreneur of the Year, and *Fast Company*'s Most Innovative Companies are considered name-brand awards. Recognition at this level can reinforce credibility with your brand for years and bring mass visibility to your company. Although most name-brand awards require a small fee to apply, they are highly competitive and undergo a rigorous judging process. Because these awards are recognizable to the general public, there is a perceived level of business status that comes with this type of recognition that translates to the way you are referred to moving forward.

Category-specific awards provide local or industry-driven recognition. There is a mixture of fee-based and free applications in this category, but you will find most of these awards are nomination-based. Category-specific awards can be your local business journal awards like Best Places to Work, Chamber of Commerce recognition, or as niche as the American Medical Association Excellence in Medicine if you are a practicing physician. When you are a finalist or win a reputable category award, you earn quick credibility with those in your niche target audience. Targeted exposure like this can drive visibility for lead flow, keep you top of mind for stakeholders, and shorten sales cycles. Awards in this category can also reinforce why a prospect should move to the next conversation with you. It also provides a sense of pride for your current customer base, giving them the thought, *We are lucky to have an opportunity to work with them.* When it comes to turbocharging referrals, which we will cover more in step 6, awards can give your referral sources a good reason to send your information over to a potential prospect. Referral sources refer to services and products that make them look good to their network at the end of the day. Remarketed award recognition does just that for your network.

There are two steps to the award application process for you as a leader. The first step is to identify the awards that would meaningfully provide value to your business and create an award calendar to monitor. This exercise can be done in several sittings alongside your team or outsourced with the right parameters. The award calendar can be kept in a calendar format, Excel sheet, or Word document. When curating this list, include the award name, link to the information, qualifications required, and nomination/application deadlines. Most awards occur annually so doing the work to curate this list on the front end will ease the process of award applications for years to come. If there are awards you come across that benefit your business, but you do not qualify for them yet due to revenue restrictions or employee count, put them on a separate list to monitor for future applications. The goal of this exercise is to create a list you can revisit at the end or beginning of every year to determine where you will focus your efforts over the next 12 months and project the application deadlines you need to reserve on your calendar. Your list of desired awards should include a mixture of name-brand recognition and category-specific awards.

Once your award calendar is finalized, creating your award submissions is the second step in the award application process. Most applications include a mixture of business stat-based and thought leadership questions. Many also include questions directed to the company's most senior leader. The way you answer these questions matters and can often be the reason you stand out against other applicants. Award applications can be extensive, so get as much of a head start on your timeline as possible to craft a thoughtful submission. A hack to accelerate your submission process is to save the Word document of your crafted responses for each application to build off of for future submissions. This will allow you to go back and analyze what could potentially be utilized for other award applications or be improved or updated for future submissions for the same award.

Judges are reviewing hundreds, if not thousands, of applications at a time for many of these awards, so you have to be strategic about how you differentiate yourself throughout this strategy. Submitting strong business stats alone will not win you an award. It's all about how you convey those successes through strong storytelling and what makes you unique that makes your application stand out. Sound familiar? The Strategic Business Influencer mindset applies when it comes to standing out in business and leadership award applications. Being more of yourself is your differentiating factor.

As you apply for awards, it is common to take several submissions until you start seeing winning recognition. It is important to learn from the past businesses that have been named winners and pay special attention to what the award organization highlights about them. This could highlight some of the story elements the judging committee seeks. Trust that you will gain traction over time that pays dividends for your business, but sometimes that means you have to start small.

Joyce Durst is the founder and CEO of Growth Acceleration Partners (GAP), a tenured consulting and technology services company with over 550 team members across the United States and Latin America. She is now a global multi-award-winning entrepreneur, but this visible recognition was not always there for her and her business. Awards were not even on the radar for her team's marketing strategy until she started being nominated for a few here and there. This is how Joyce and her team started down the path of award submissions for Growth Acceleration Partners:

We stumbled upon awards several years ago. For the first few awards we applied for, we did not source them for ourselves. We were first exposed to awards when an industry peer or customer nominated us for them. It was a surprise and honor to be nominated for these awards. But as we started becoming finalists and even winning some of these awards, one of the things that certainly I noticed and our marketing team noticed was that it put our company's name out to a broader audience of people that I might not have ever connected with. As a small company trying to grow and become a large company, we had very limited resources. We are a fully bootstrapped company, which is rare in our industry, and we do not have the budget to allocate to marketing that a lot of our larger competitors do. Once we saw the value awards could bring us, we decided to continue pursuing awards to get more awareness for the company.[4]

As Joyce's company, GAP, continued to scale and surpass new business milestones, she found her team was not progressing with bigger award recognition even though her company had well surpassed the required qualifications. She saw other companies and leaders win these more recognized awards who were well deserving in their own right, but many had not accomplished near the growth her team at GAP had achieved in a short amount of time. This pursuit was not a self-serving one for Joyce. Being a self-proclaimed introvert, she shies away from personal recognition. She saw it as an opportunity to gain recognition for her hardworking team and as a PR strategy to give her visibility she otherwise could not afford. Although Joyce's company was growing rapidly, it took almost three to four years before she started to win awards she had been applying for year after year. Joyce described the moment it all clicked for her:

We won some smaller awards that were exciting, but it really was a learning process to develop strong award applications. Looking back now, the mistakes we made in the beginning make me laugh because they make total sense. I ended up learning about the mistakes I was making in the application process because judges that we had had in various award applications would call me after, which I am very grateful they did. They would tell me we should have won this and that award. Judges would tell me they were familiar with my success, and know how successful the company was but that my application was terrible.

I just could not figure out what was so terrible about my application. I always put in our applications the impressive growth percentages and all the great brand-name customers we had acquired. I did not understand how any of that information could read as terrible. I finally had one judge lay it all out for me. He told me the truth was it sounded like an engineer wrote my application. The humor is I am an engineer, and I was the one writing the application. All the facts and figures were there, but there was no story. It was not connecting with people, which is what you have to do to stand out. So I had to start thinking about telling our story how our customers see it. As soon as I finally got that through my engineering thick skull, it was magic! I learned to write our applications in an entirely different way. We are still factual and include our business stats, but we focus on sharing those metrics through our stories, mission, and impact. This is what makes an application memorable.

It is funny because my team says all I do is tell stories when I get in front of the team to talk about our vision, lessons learned, and successes. I looked at the award applications more like a test, where I was supposed to just put down the right answer. But in reality, it was not a test at all. What it shifted to was conveying the storytelling I was already doing behind the scenes with my team throughout the application process.[5]

Since Joyce and her team made this shift in award applications, she has won the EY Entrepreneur of the Year Gulf South Award, been listed on the Inc. 5000, Most Promising Microsoft Solutions Providers, named one of the 2024 Women in Business, and inducted into the Austin Tech Hall of Fame, among many other honors. She has found gaining traction with awards has changed how she is now introduced on stages and through referrals. People like including in her introduction some of the awards her team has been recognized for, which she finds gives her instant credibility with people who do not know her yet. Joyce has also noticed that when GAP remarkets the awards they have won, there is a spike in referrals sent her way. When her audience sees they've won a new award, it serves as a reminder for those who want to recommend her team. Once people are recommended to her, awards also enhance her sales process with prospects:

> *If anybody is gonna work with us, they are going to google the company, and they are going to google me. The awards that appear in my Google search put us ahead of many competitors we are working to win the business against. It makes a prospect feel great about working with our company, and they become excited that they have the opportunity to work with us. Winning awards is also significant to employees. Everyone wants to share with friends and family thay they work for one of the top companies in their industry. These honors are a great way to recognize the important contributions the team has made. Awards have given us an amount of publicity we could have never been able to afford in our marketing budget.[6]*

Joyce and her team have continued to narrow down the awards that provide meaningful value based on their business's current objectives. They now apply for about five awards per year. Awards are not meant to be a volume play, and frankly, good applications can't be. Her team has found that going through the award application processes forces you to step back and analyze how strong you and the company are in each of the areas being reviewed. It is a great exercise to determine if your company is delivering on the promises you set forth in your vision. When you create your award calendar, prioritize which awards are attainable and provide the most value. Focus your time on creating a compelling application for those select awards and learn from the process. It takes iteration, authenticity, and resilience to reap the benefits awards can strategically bring your business.

TAKING THE STAGE AS A THOUGHT LEADER

Not every Strategic Business Influencer does public speaking, and that's perfectly okay. It's optional for reaching your influence goals. However, if you enjoy educating others about your area of expertise, and if you have a knack for it, public speaking can be an incredibly effective PR strategy to enhance your lead generation and credibility.

Just like media coverage, targeted speaking engagements can drive name recognition within your industry. You can share your knowledge, engage audiences through storytelling, and ultimately leave them more knowledgeable than when they walked in the door. Don't focus on selling your products or services; your goal should be to provide actionable insights that your audience will appreciate, to generate goodwill. Actual selling can come later.

If you manage to land a speaking opportunity, even an unpaid one, one of the best things you can do is capture digital video and photos of yourself in front of the group. Visuals are key when it comes to remarketing your talks. A photo of yourself doing public speaking will make a great header photo for your LinkedIn page and an extra visual for the "About" page of your website. There's something about seeing someone in front of a group, no matter how big or small, that conveys expertise and thought leadership. When you're in a position where you can teach others, you naturally earn the trust and respect of your audience.

It's important to leverage strategic remarketing to maximize the value of your speaking engagements. Just as with other forms of PR, simply participating in speaking engagements won't give you the full impact you're looking for. By strategically repurposing your speaking content and visuals, you can increase your reach and reinforce your credibility.

How Dr. Tammie Chang Built Her Influence with PR

Board-certified pediatric oncologist Dr. Tammie Chang faced debilitating burnout at a critical point in her career when she lost all sense of self outside of her work. After recovering from a low point that brought her close to suicide, she was determined to help other women in medicine who faced similar crises. She heard story after story of doctors facing lonely journeys with little or no support. In response, Dr. Chang started two ventures focused on coaching women physicians and providing a strong support group.

She then wrote an inspirational book about her own crisis and how she survived it, hoping to use the book to advocate for cultural change in healthcare. As her publication date approached, Dr. Chang needed a PR strategy to scale up the community she had already established and to reach as many physicians as possible. She planned a well-rounded campaign that blended brand-name consumer media with targeted micromedia to raise her visibility and credibility within the medical community. It was important to balance how her story was told, to make sure she was reaching the right audiences who had the power to make an impact within healthcare.

Within a year, Dr. Chang had shared her story with the following media outlets—both niche and mainstream—among others:

- KevinMD, a physician-run website that targets other physicians, ran an excerpt from the book to its 510,000 unique monthly visitors.
- *Becker's Healthcare Podcast* featured Dr. Chang on their "Women's Leadership" program. This podcast targets hospital

administrators and executives and reaches more than 50,000 listeners per month.

- *Medical Economics*, the leading healthcare business publication for physicians, asked Dr. Chang to contribute two articles, which became visible to more than 140,000 unique monthly visitors.

- Arianna Huffington's Thrive Global ran an excerpt from the book about the burnout epidemic, reaching more than 940,000 unique monthly visitors.

- The popular Oprah Daily website, which reaches 9.35 million unique monthly visitors, most of them women, ran an interview with Dr. Chang on how to live life to the fullest.

- *Harvard Business Review*, the iconic management outlet that reaches 9.6 million unique monthly visitors, featured an original article by Dr. Chang on how physicians are overcoming burnout.

These examples are just some of the ways she could share her story and impact. Within a year, she had reached podcast audiences totaling 126,000 listeners and website audiences totaling *182 million* unique monthly visitors. As you can see, she landed a balanced combination of some outlets that everyone can recognize and others that would only be recognized by her fellow physicians. That combination helped her grow both her platform of fans and her credibility within her profession.

As she continued to grow her visibility, Dr. Chang applied to share her courageous story as a TEDx talk and was accepted. As with all the other media she had generated, the biggest impact wasn't on the audience in front of her but on the far larger online audience she could reach with online remarketing. The video of her talk about women doctors struggling in silence was viewed more than 51,000 times.

Dr. Chang's book *Boundaries for Women Physicians* became an Amazon bestseller in 16 different subcategories. More than a year later, she continues to grow her following as a thought leader. By blending micromedia, brand-name media, public speaking, and strategic retargeting, she has become a Strategic Business Influencer for exactly the audience she was seeking.

HOW TO DO "SMARTPHONE PR"

While clients like Jack Aspenson and Tammie Chang benefited greatly by hiring a qualified and experienced PR firm, the reality is that you *don't* need to sink a lot of money into such a firm to begin getting media opportunities. You can get a campaign off the ground on your own, with just a smartphone, if you're willing to invest your time rather than your money.

As recently as 10 years ago, smartphones and social media weren't powerful enough to make such an approach possible; clients depended on PR professionals with the right connections and skills to drive effective outreach. But today the range of available tools and resources is truly astonishing. Regardless of your background or budget, you can begin to build relationships with key micromedia creators in your field.

As an aspiring Strategic Business Influencer, you need to stay up-to-date with industry news and other experts in your field. Take the time to identify the journalists, writers, podcasters, YouTubers, and other content creators who cover your area of expertise. This should include full-time journalists who cover specific beats for a single publication, as well as freelance contributors whose work appears in multiple outlets. Most publications have drastically reduced their full-time staff and are now far more reliant on freelancers.

Once you've identified these targeted media members, start following them on the social platforms where they are active. By engaging with their content (liking, sharing, and commenting) you can begin to build relationships and establish yourself as a reliable voice in your field. Look for opportunities to share useful thoughts or supplemental information on their articles, podcasts, or videos. Say nice things about whatever aspects you found most valuable.

Remember, your goal at this point is to start a conversation and build rapport with these key media figures, *not* to pitch them. By consistently engaging with their content, you'll get on their radar and increase the likelihood of them seeking you out for your opinions.

For instance, I did an executive brand audit and consultation for the chief investment officer of a capital investment firm. When I saw that he was frequently quoted in major outlets such as the *Wall Street Journal*, I complimented his company's PR team for doing a great job. He replied that his company didn't have a PR team; he had garnered all of this exposure himself. He never cold-pitched journalists, but merely followed key media people on LinkedIn and commented on their stories. This strategy had led to consistent dialogue with several key outlets, driven entirely via social media.

This executive's LinkedIn profile showcased his impressive credentials and expertise, so any journalists who clicked on his profile would immediately see that he knew what he was talking about as a professional investor. They started reaching out to him for comments on whatever stories they were working on. It may sound paradoxical, but journalists who get literally hundreds of email pitches per day may ignore them all and seek out their own experts to help fill their articles. By offering value to the financial media without asking for anything in return, he began to get an exceptional amount of attention, boosting his visibility and credibility nationwide.

Keep in mind that today's media professionals are usually overworked, underpaid, and facing constant pressure to keep up with the never-ending flood of all kinds of content. They are looking for thought leaders who will save them time and make their jobs easier by providing reliable information and expert opinions. By differentiating yourself and building direct, organic relationships, you can achieve exceptional PR results—even without a professional PR team.

Journalists, pundits, and podcast hosts receive thousands of pitches every week, so they have their guard up and their BS detectors on high alert whenever they open an email. But when tagged by name on their social media content, they're just like the rest of us. They want to see how their audience is reacting to their latest offering, and they're pleased to find thoughtful commentary and sincere compliments.

Another effective way to drive your own publicity is by subscribing to journalist inquiry platforms such as Qwoted and ProfNet. These platforms have transformed public relations by enabling journalists to post inquiries for subject matter experts for the specific stories they're working on. Subscribing to these platforms ensures that media opportunities you qualify for will be delivered directly to your inbox. Both mainstream journalists and targeted micromedia writers and podcasters utilize these platforms to find qualified experts.

If you spot a request that's in your strike zone, it's crucial to respond promptly and answer the questions presented without wandering off-topic. Journalists usually work on tight deadlines, and they will be grateful for information that's prompt, accurate, and tailored to their specific story. This is not the time to promote your company; this is the time to build new relationships by being extremely helpful. Play the long game, knowing that some of the assistance you give journalists today will turn into good karma in the future. They might come back to you repeatedly for your expertise.

UPGRADING FROM SMARTPHONE PR TO PROFESSIONAL PR

As we've just seen, there are now some amazing opportunities to act as your own publicist, offering your expertise directly to journalists and pundits who will appreciate it. This leads to an obvious question: If smartphone PR is so powerful, why should anyone hire a professional publicist?

The choice of do-it-yourself PR versus professional PR should be determined by a combination of your financial resources, your available time, and your timeline for reaching your goals. For most entrepreneurs, this decision comes down to how they want to allocate their limited marketing budget. If money is tight, every dollar you spend on a PR campaign is one less dollar available for ads on Google, Facebook, or wherever else you've been getting the best bang for your advertising.

You also need to consider what type of results you are looking for and where it makes the most sense to allocate limited resources to reach those goals. If you're primarily focused on *short-term* lead generation within a fixed geographic area, paid advertising is probably the right place to direct your budget. You can do self-generated PR (or hand it off to an enterprising staffer) and see how far you can get by making your thought leadership available to journalists and content creators.

On the other hand, if your goals are building credibility and visibility within your industry and boosting consistent, *long-term* lead generation, consider investing a portion of your marketing budget into a professional PR campaign. For most Strategic Business Influencers, PR efforts can take months or even years to fully pay off. You may not have the time and energy required, week after week, to do an outstanding job of smartphone PR. Investing in high-quality outside support can provide a type of long-term impact that levels the playing field against your bigger competitors.

Even if—especially if—you've started to build a sporadic media presence via self-generated publicity, partnering with the right PR firm can help you scale up your efforts and maintain consistency. You'll be able to focus your time and energy on developing ideas, writing articles, and doing interviews while your PR firm handles outreach to the media.

When searching for a PR firm, don't hire the first one that offers to work with you. They should be interviewing you with as much of a critical eye as you are interviewing them. Be wary of any PR firm that guarantees amazing coverage because garnering true earned media is hard and unpredictable. Ask what types of media outlets they would potentially pitch and what they consider reasonable expectations for the outcome. Ask what coverage they've garnered recently for their other clients.

If you decide to go forward with a publicist or PR firm, make sure you're completely aligned about your niche target audiences and the kinds of micromedia they consume. Nothing is more frustrating than realizing that you and your PR firm have a fundamental disagreement about goals and strategies—*after* they've already put weeks or months into a campaign.

IT'S A MARATHON, NOT A SPRINT

As you navigate the challenging world of PR as an aspiring Strategic Business Influencer, never forget that the name of the game is building credibility and trust. Whether you are doing it alone or working with a professional team, embrace micromedia and then leverage it via digital word-of-mouth to showcase your expertise.

Above all, remember that successful business PR is a marathon, not a sprint. You won't get one magic piece of media coverage that instantly makes you and your company famous. But if you focus on consistent targeting of the right micromedia in the right niches, your profile should begin to rise with those audiences over time.

Please also remember that your target audience is just as swamped as you are. Every day, their email inboxes fill up with more newsletters, their social media feeds are overflowing, and they might be downloading more podcasts than they can possibly listen to. Like you, they need to be increasingly selective about which content they spend their precious time consuming. So it's more crucial than ever for you to deliver quality content. Like journalists, regular people won't continue to pay attention if their early experiences with your material are negative.

The good news, however, is that PR is very different than it was even 10 years ago. You now have an unprecedented ability to level the playing field against your bigger, deep-pocketed competitors. By using a targeted strategy, Strategic Business Influencers gain a competitive advantage over those who still cling to an outdated approach to PR. They can build a great reputation, attract the right potential customers and investors, and generally maximize their visibility and clout.

Speaking of great content, in the next step, we'll explore what it means to have a smart content strategy, so you'll have plenty of high-quality material to use in your PR campaigns.

Step 5

DEVELOP CONTENT THAT DRIVES LEADS

I am frustrated with my marketing team because our business page gets almost no engagement on social media. Their content strategy is just not working and I'm honestly skeptical whether social media is even worth our time."

Does this frustration feel familiar to you?

This is a statement I hear at least one CEO express at every workshop I conduct. It is frustrating when you have deployed valuable resources into creating content and you see other people seemingly winning while you battle to get 5 to 10 likes on a post.

"What am I missing?" is one of the most common questions I get asked.

Do you know how to track if the content produces results for your business? All you can visibly see are the three likes on your last company page LinkedIn post. So, something is not working, right? You are right, but the issue might not be what you think it is.

Content in today's environment is no longer a simple equation. Often, it is not just the content strategy that is the issue; it is also the content deployment. There are two barriers when it comes to the deployment of content for companies. The first barrier is the lack of trust consumers have with content that is produced and published by companies. Consumers immediately know when they see content from a company in which the end goal is a product or service sale. With that perception, it is hard for companies to get past that subconscious understanding, no matter how entertaining their content is. When it comes to social media, the second barrier companies face is that the algorithm for a business page is not in your favor due to the platform's business model. Social media channels are businesses, and the way they make money is by letting a business have access to users on their platform through advertising. So the likelihood of you being able to consistently garner visibility through your business page on social media is low because those channels will not give you visibility for free in their algorithm. They ultimately want you to pay for access to their audience through an advertising campaign. You can have a successful advertising campaign strategy online, but once you start, it can be hard to turn it off because the algorithm works to keep you feeding Google or a social media platform more dollars. So, before jumping into an advertising campaign, make sure this is where you can best spend your dollars in the long term. Many small to medium-sized businesses are not ready to make that commitment. If you are trying to communicate a message through your corporate brand, it is increasingly not being heard due to cost and trust barriers. You need to be the messenger.

Leveraging your brand as a Strategic Business Influencer allows you to break down these two barriers in content marketing. Refine Labs conducted a study on LinkedIn that showed personal LinkedIn profiles received 2.75 times the impressions and five times more engagement than corporate LinkedIn profiles.[1] This is not only because algorithms give more visibility to people than companies, but consumers want to engage with people versus logos. Leveraging your brand in content marketing as the leader of your company allows you to circumvent these pitfalls that are tough for businesses to overcome and often costly. There are three things that typically keep leaders from deploying a content strategy alongside their company.

1. Feeling that producing content marketing is not worth their time.
2. Fearing that they need to present an inauthentic personality online.
3. Concern that too much personal visibility will devalue the company (i.e., "If I get visible, clients will only want to work with me!").

Each concern is a dated mindset that limits a leader's impact and the company's growth. The upside of being a leader supporting your company's content strategy is that it allows you to bring more scalability to what you are already doing behind the scenes. As a leader, you are already teaching, building meaningful relationships, having strategic conversations, and telling stories that move the needle.

Let's just do it all more at scale.

With the right content strategy, you will accelerate key responsibilities like building trust for your business, relationship-building, customer communication, education, sharing your vision, and talent recruitment. The ability to do this at scale will result in shorter sales cycles, customer loyalty, qualified lead generation, top talent acquisition, and employee engagement. Deploying a content strategy will take you beyond limiting one-on-one interactions and give you more opportunities to connect directly with your customers, partners, employees, and investors.

HOW CONTENT IS CONSUMED

There was once a time when content consumption only came from mediums such as TV news segments, the radio, and newspapers. These traditional channels were heavily relied upon because they were the only way to disseminate information to the mass public. In this previous environment, newsrooms had all the control over whose voice and what message got out there. With the rise of the internet, email, blogs, podcasts, and social media channels, there ultimately became more content share of voice. People and companies no longer needed to break through the gatekeepers of the newsrooms. We have now found ourselves in a more crowdsourced approach to content that is consumed rather than outsourced. This means more content from more sources. Over time, this dynamic has resulted in audiences shifting their attention from traditional content mediums toward the sources themselves, the subject matter experts. Over half of the US population consumes their news on social media versus traditional mediums, according to research conducted by the Pew Research Center.[2] Pew also found in their study that traditional reporters were often not the source people were consuming their news from online. People seek trust, firsthand accounts, perspective, and experience over mass media. I want you to ask yourself, who is the trusted source right now for your industry? It should be you.

BUT WHERE DO I FIND THE TIME?

When you are in the trenches of growing a business, time is a currency, and frankly, you do not have enough of it. This is why most leaders need to pay more attention to content creation for their personal platforms. It can feel almost impossible to keep up with the corporate brand content churn and demanding day-to-day business tasks. As a leader, you must constantly evaluate if where you are spending your time is yielding results and rewards. In this chapter, I will not ask you to put all your effort into being on four social media platforms, posting five times a week, hosting a podcast, and sending email newsletters. If I'm being frank, much of that is not worth your time. My goal with this book is to help you prioritize your time on what you do best as a leader, bringing visibility to the strengths that drive your company forward, even those that usually happen behind the scenes. Your presence as a Strategic Business Influencer online has to be authentic to serve your company well, and posting every day might not be realistic for a leader in your industry. That is okay. There are no magic rules or formulas when it comes to how often you should post or the amount of platforms you should be on. Success in building your brand as a Strategic Business Influencer comes from defining what is the highest and best use of your time. That comes with understanding three questions.

- What outcomes do you want your content to achieve?
- What type of content does your audience value?
- Where does your audience spend their time?

It is more important for you to master these three questions than to produce a high content volume. As you reflect on these questions, I encourage you to identify one to two areas to focus your time on for maximum return.

The outcomes you want your content to achieve can change as your business grows. There might be a season when prospect lead generation is a higher priority than talent acquisition. If you have a marketing or leadership team, this is where you can build alignment to know where you can best support. Understanding the type of content your audience values requires listening first. Think through the pain points your audience faces, the type of industry news they are consuming, and the format of content they will most likely consume. Some industries might do better with short-form content versus long-form, video, or audio. The question of where your audience spends their time should be addressed last. This is easier to nail down once the first two questions are answered. You want to focus on where your presence online as a Strategic Business Influencer could generate the strongest results. For most leaders, this means focusing on one social media platform and opportunities to support corporate brand content assets such as email marketing and press opportunities. Your brand needs to stay targeted and impactful with your content strategy. The mistake I see a lot of leaders make is they try to be on all channels and diminish the impact they could have on their brand and the corporate brand. This approach also burns time and resources more quickly, resulting in leaders abandoning their presence online. It is more important to execute one channel well than to have a presence on multiple channels you are trying to grow if time and resources do not allow.

As you answer the three questions above, I encourage you to keep your Influence ID in mind. It will provide guardrails to keep you focused on what is authentic and the best use of your time, energy, and resources. Do not feel the need to drive content with formats that feel completely out of your comfort zone. For example, if video is daunting, stick to written or audio content. You want to enjoy the content creation process and avoid coming across as inauthentic. A common misconception is that you need highly produced video or photo assets to post online. While those can be great, studies have found that phone-recorded visual assets have garnered more engagement because they feel more authentic to an audience.[3] What generates results is not the format of content; it is a value-driven mindset with content creation. That is the competitive advantage of a Strategic Business Influencer—you can lead as someone who is there purely to educate versus sell a product or service. This approach accelerates trust, engagement, and referrals, which we will dive more into in the next step.

MASTERING YOUR CONTENT STRATEGY

For Strategic Business Influencers, content should not be measured on vanity metrics such as likes, impressions, and engagement. Your content strategy should be measured on the results it drives for your business. This could be new partnerships, heightened deal flow, shorter sales cycles, or quality of employee candidates. Approaching your content with this mindset helps you zero in on where to lean in strategically—so you're spending your time where it drives the highest return. Your job as a Strategic Business Influencer is to bring the right visibility to what you are doing day-to-day as your industry's leader. To establish yourself as the go-to leader in your industry, center your content strategy around bringing visibility to these three areas.

1. Leading as the visionary
2. Leading as the educator
3. Leading as the relationship-builder

I imagine these areas of leadership feel second nature and align with where you are already investing your time or *hoping* to spend it. Lean on these areas you know to drive your content creation.

Leading as the Visionary

It can be argued that your primary role as a leader is to cast and communicate vision consistently, inspiring others to rally around it. The same applies when it comes to gathering a community around your content. When articulating a powerful vision, it involves sharing the story of where you came from, the work you are doing now, and, most importantly, why you are on a journey to reach your vision. Megan Gluth, the CEO of Catalynt you read about in step 2, shared a different way she approaches thinking about content to keep it mission-minded:

I realized I do not get to judge whether my thought leadership commentary is wise or useful. All I have control over is ensuring I get what I believe can be impactful out into the world. Other people who read or hear my thoughts get to say whether it is wise or useful to them. As long as I remember the mission, it is a lot easier for me to create content.[4]

This category of content can be most engaging because, when done right, it often can be viewed as the most authentic, as Megan mentioned. The challenge with this category is that many leaders tend to fill their LinkedIn profiles and email marketing with this content category because it is second nature to them. After all, you are getting to talk about your passion. This content category can be challenging, though, if you are just starting to build your brand. When you are not well known, your audience might not fully recognize your value yet. As you build your brand, it is wise to use this type of content sparingly. You want to walk a fine line by sharing your story and vision without coming across as overly promotional. When lightly integrated into your content strategy, this area of content can often be a strong opportunity for connection with your audience. This category of content can consist of sharing the following with your audience.

- Your entrepreneurial story
- Your framework
- Your intellectual property
- Your mission
- Your values
- A behind-the-scenes look at your day-to-day
- Company news and celebrations

Earlier, I shared Sarah Dusek's story. She is an award-winning entrepreneur and cofounder of Enygma Ventures. Sarah's entrepreneurial experience was vital to serve her mission of making entrepreneurship more approachable, accessible, and less intimidating for women. Through her stories, she was able to relate to women who were facing self-doubt and working to overcome impostor syndrome. Sarah was generous with sharing her experiences through stories she would post on LinkedIn, newsletters, speaking events, articles, and podcasts. She utilized her content to extend her impact beyond what she could achieve one-on-one with the entrepreneurs in her fund. As traction around her stories and experiences grew with her audience, Sarah was presented with the opportunity to tell her story and vision to many when a publisher offered her a book deal. Her book, *Thinking Bigger*, ultimately became a movement for women to challenge the limits they set for themselves. This opportunity for Sarah resulted from the time and dedication she put into consistently sharing her vision and experience to better women in the entrepreneurial community.

Since we covered what works well for this content category, let's now talk about what to avoid. If this is the only part of your leadership you bring visibility to, your content results will grow stagnant over time. Think of what happens when you are scrolling through your LinkedIn newsfeed, and you feel like you are seeing ad after ad. You start to feel the value of LinkedIn decrease in your mind. When filling your platform with too much visionary content, it can begin to feel like you are constantly using your platform to push your agenda. As a leader, you want to avoid content that looks like it is serving you more than your audience. To avoid this, be mindful of the frequency of content you should be publishing in this category. It should be impactful while being the smallest content category in your arsenal.

Being the Educator

I believe successful entrepreneurs have to be good teachers to inspire great leadership. Many entrepreneurs I know truly find fulfillment in educating on what they are passionate about. You are most likely already conversing with your team, peers, and clients, sharing your analysis on trends you are seeing, industry news, and timely events. Your perspective from these conversations is what we want to bring more visibility to in this category of content. The ability to position yourself online as the subject matter expert in your industry starts to build influence that can scale your influence quickly with your target audience. With this content category, it is important to understand what news stories and timely topics your audience is currently paying attention to. To master this content category, craft your content around your analysis of the four types of educator content.

Seasonal Content

The advantage of seasonal content is you can pre-plan when and how this type of content should be integrated into your strategy. Although it might not drive a lot of new visibility, it will strongly resonate and spur action with your current audience. As you look at the next 12 months, take note of timely events that typically impact your audience. It can vary depending on your industry but can include holidays, weather, customer cycles, or industry deadlines. Once you have those dates marked, your plan should align to craft content that will speak to those events that are already top of mind for your target audience. For example, if you are a leadership consultant, you know a high-priority time of year for leaders is during the annual planning season, which tends to fall in Q4 for most companies. Anticipating your audience's needs during these events will keep you and your brand on the offense, and you will build a plan that integrates timely content year after year.

Newsjacking Content

The British Geological Survey (BGS), a company that monitors earthquakes across the United Kingdom, is not typically in the news, but it had one of the leading headlines in *TIME* magazine and the BBC in 2024. The ironic thing about this story was that their scientists were not featured talking about the country's earthquake magnitudes or after-shocks per se. The organization's feature in *TIME* magazine was tied to a story everyone across the globe had been following that year: Taylor Swift's Eras Tour.

The group utilized the over 200,000 people visiting from around the globe to gather seismic data from the three-day event. The unique head-line in BBC read, "Taylor Swift Fans Make the Earth Move at Edinburgh Gig." Since their monitoring stations were within close proximity to the stadium Taylor Swift played in Scotland, the British Geological Survey and its seismologists used the series of concerts at the nearby stadium to conduct proprietary research to measure the crowd reactions during the three-hour-long setlist. The experts shared that the seismic activity peaked during her song "Ready for It?" and was the strongest during her Friday show in Edinburgh, citing the fans created a whopping 80 kW of power during the song. This coverage led to similar stories for her Seattle and Los Angeles concerts. The data collected not only landed an article for the organization in the BBC, but it also led to a video interview with *TIME* magazine featuring their volcanologist who attended the concert as part of the research. The timing of this story and the clever study led to global coverage of the British Geological Survey in media outlets such as CBS News, the *Washington Post, Billboard*, CNN, Page Six, MSN, and Reuters. This exposure provided a higher level of discoverability and awareness of what the British Geological Survey team does for the United Kingdom. The reality is that the national organization would have never been able to get global press coverage like this unless a catastrophic event occurred. Luckily, the team's quick idea to lean on their expertise and tie it to one of the most talked-about events in the world allowed them to leverage the moment to create unlikely visibility in an entertaining way. The team of scientists successfully linked their expertise to one of the year's most timely events, creating significant gains for a brand lacking the opportunity to create visibility any other day on an international stage. The intentionality of this strategy centered around the art of what is known as newsjacking.

Marketing pioneer and bestselling author David Meerman Scott coined the term "newsjacking" in 2011 and described it as "the art and science of injecting your ideas into a breaking news story so you and your ideas get noticed."[5] When the art of newsjacking is mastered, this is often the content that can drive the most attention from an audience already following you and drive visibility for your target audience to discover you. Think about this category of content as meeting your audience where they are. Your ability to deliver timely content that connects to a current event or news story your audience is paying attention to can increase engagement and open rates regarding email marketing. This allows your audience to start viewing you not only as an industry expert but also as an industry news source. This shift in your audience's mind drives anticipation and repeat content viewership. The news you comment on can be anything from new studies to national, local, or industry-specific news. It can be a niche topic and still drive tremendous impact with the right story your target audience has their attention on. Paying attention to this category can also safeguard your brand reputation. It is important to watch the news cycle to ensure the content you are putting out does not come across as tone-deaf. We have all seen the mishaps of what can happen quickly online when leaders ignore news events or send the wrong message at the wrong time.

Event-Driven Content

One of the best ways to magnify your impact and presence at an event is by leveraging your experience to create content. Typically, industry conferences are packed with education that can be valuable to your audience. Sharing takeaways from your event experience and tagging the event or utilizing the event hashtag gives your content a higher likelihood of being discovered by others who were in attendance or following the event online. The goal of this category of content is to bring the networking that happens at physical events into a digital connection point to nurture the relationship over time. Event-driven content can broaden your exposure and network with the right audience if the content that is shared drives insights and meaningful engagement. We will also look at the impact event-driven content can have on relationship-building as well in the following section.

On-Trend Content

On-trend content might have you a bit apprehensive if you are not in the know about the latest social media trends. I promise this does not require you to learn the latest social media dance craze. With on-trend content, you give your audience either a forecast or an analysis of the industry trends you see. Jack, the founder of S3 Surface Solutions, saw the writing on the wall post-COVID and predicted a transportation shortage that would impact the entire manufacturing industry. This led him to strategically order trucks full of products preemptively to avoid delays and S3 product shortages. It was a risk many on his team and industry were not fully confident in. Although risky, Jack's decision paid off when they became the only manufacturer during that time that did not experience shortages that caused other companies to experience delays, layoffs, and a decrease in revenue. Jack still shares lessons learned through his content and podcast interviews from that moment from the leading indicators he saw that led him to make a decision of calculated risk that paid off. He always explains what trends he is looking at in case they can impact another entrepreneur's decision to make a strategic choice that could change the course of their business. Jack is quick to point out that not all risky decisions entrepreneurs have to make are successful, but underscores the importance of sharing with other aspiring entrepreneurs and peers what he learns from the ones that are and are not. In Jack's case, he is not influencing a large audience, but he is influencing the very niche categories his businesses serve. He believes if he can keep his focus on the industries he serves, he can "impact greater communities by keeping them healthy and protected." This is why Jack's education in content is important for his company's visibility, but more importantly, it has an overall impact on his mission with the community.

If not executed responsibly, some of these forms of content can cause unnecessary friction for you and your business. Avoid getting sucked into hot-button topics if it will not further your impact or mission. The urge to do this almost always serves as a reaction and usually only provides you with personal satisfaction short-term. What this reaction can create is an unnecessary breeding ground of divisiveness on your platform. All that chalks up to at the end of the day is you and your business losing long-term with one side of the issue. There are instances in certain industries when leaders must get involved in timely, controversial conversations where issues like legislation will impact how they do business. If you must address a hot-button issue on your platform, the best way to do this is by leaning in as an educator versus a dictator. This will allow you to frame the conversation in a way that builds trust and fosters open-mindedness as best as possible with your audience.

Being the Relationship-Builder

Great entrepreneurs know how to build strong relationships. The ability to create and foster the right relationships is the cornerstone of what provides an initial launching pad for businesses. If you reflect on your time in business, I imagine you can trace your successes to key relationships you have built over time. This is why relationship-building is a vital component of a leader's responsibilities. Leaders must create an ecosystem of relationships surrounding their business to influence prospects, vendors, employees, and investors. Throughout your career, most of your relationships may have started or grown through events and in-person interactions. Gone are the days when you must rely on the next networking event or time you can get on someone's calendar for coffee or lunch to initiate or grow relationships. Now you can create and influence relationships through online interactions with event-driven, recognition, and spotlight content opportunities. We will dive into exactly how to curate relationships at scale online in our next step through an interview series.

Event-Driven Content

To dive deeper into event-driven interactions, content can be utilized to foster touchpoints over time with individuals you have met through networking events or conferences. This requires the same skills as keeping a connection in person. Each interaction should be about getting an update on what they have been up to, what challenges they are facing, and understanding how you might be able to support them. Posting a comment on the thread with their latest update, tagging them in articles you believe they will benefit from, and replying to their latest email newsletter allows you to foster this connection over time and keeps the relationship top of mind.

Recognition Shares

It's not a surprise that a 2024 Gallup study found that the most memorable recognition for employees came from the company's CEO.[6] As your business grows, finding ways to recognize your high-performing team members online allows you to create meaningful connection points with them. Crafting internal newsletters and social media posts recognizing wins can include posting or commenting on the following.

- New hire announcements
- Celebrating promotions
- Spotlighting an employee's work

- Company anniversaries
- Celebrating life milestones such as a birthday, marriage, or new addition to the family

Recognizing team members on a public platform can drive company loyalty and showcase culture to prospective employees. You can also take the same approach to publicly recognize vendors, partners, and clients on your platforms. It is human nature to appreciate those who give us recognition, which goes a long way in solidifying relationships.

Spotlight Content

The ability to take the spotlight off of you and shine it on someone else is a way to build goodwill at scale in your content strategy. To achieve this, look for opportunities to utilize formats that naturally lend a spotlight to others. This can be as simple as reposting content from a client once a week to spotlight what they are doing in their community. Additional ways to create opportunities to spotlight others is inviting them on to your podcast and interviewing them, including them in the latest article you are writing for *Fast Company*, or interviewing them to feature their story in your upcoming book. Once you have a format in mind, keep your spotlights consistent monthly to further the fruits born from relationship-building with intentionality. Creating a series of regular spotlights in your content allows you to get your foot in the door to be introduced to new relationships and is a way to build affinity for current relationships. Asking to involve others in your content creates a win in their mind as well. This extension of your platform will keep you top of mind for referral opportunities. Involving others in your content also brings additional perspective and value to your audience.

Bringing relationship-building into your content strategy can be the best way to scale the impact relationships can have on your leadership and business. This is a high-reward, low-risk content category that

Strategic Business Influencers take full advantage of. Not only does it allow you to maximize reach with your time, but it also increases the number of touchpoints you have to grow trust more quickly than the traditional in-person approach. Leaders who utilize content just to be seen online versus content that bridges a relationship-building gap ultimately limit their influence online.

YOUR CONTENT CALL-TO-ACTION

Crafting content that attracts high perceived value with your audience is only one side of the content strategy equation. The ability to drive your audience to engage further with a clear call-to-action is when you start generating true traction. Remember, your goal is not to push a sale. Most audiences will not be ready to buy after consuming one piece of content. Your priority is simple: educate, build trust, and nurture. You must craft the right message that spurs your audience to take action by navigating from the platform they initially saw your content on to completing the lead magnet on your website, as we discussed in step 3. Then, have the data to create a strong follow-up nurture strategy. For example, Lisa Sun has brilliantly used the below call-to-action for her Confidence Language quiz, which has grown her email list to over 20,000 people in less than a year.

"Do I really have superpowers? This is a question I am often asked. That is why I created a quiz women could take for free to uncover their strengths and talents. Take the MyConfidence Language.com quiz and discover how powerful you are. (It's also fun with friends, family, and colleagues—a chance to celebrate all the strengths around us!)"

Another thing Lisa did well in her call-to-action was to encourage a secondary call-to-action to share her lead magnet with others. This creates a ripple effect with word-of-mouth and encourages her audience to keep others in mind who could find the lead magnet valuable.

Can I Use AI to Write My Content?

When it comes to content creation, many like to paint AI as the big bad wolf. As of the writing of this book, there are still, at times, ways to identify content generated by AI. I do not believe this will be the case 12 to 18 months from now. AI is advancing rapidly and will only become less detectable as leaders become more knowledgeable about training it more effectively.[7] This means there will be increased accessibility to generating frequent and meticulously crafted content. There was a time when leaders who were putting content out, no matter the type of content, garnered more visibility simply because they could be consistently top of mind. The loudest person in the room no longer wins because the volume notch has been dialed up on every platform. When trained properly, AI-generated content can be indistinguishable from human-written content. But just because content sounds human does not mean it drives results for your business. AI has to be met and led with the right strategy to drive results at scale by bringing visibility to what you are doing behind the scenes as a leader. So, in theory, yes, I believe you can and should, at times, utilize AI-generated content when properly trained on your voice and industry. The caveat is AI will never be able to replicate what you do daily to build differentiation with your leadership. This is why AI has to be led with your strategy of bringing visibility to the right content categories to drive results.

IT IS NOT ALL ABOUT YOU

Many leaders I speak with get stuck in creating content because they feel the weight is on them to constantly have something new to say in every piece. Leaders are often held back by the debilitating thought: *Do I have anything profound to add to the discussion, or will people think my thoughts are too basic?*

Has this type of thought prevented you from creating content in the past?

I hear this often from leaders who think their audience already knows what they would teach them or could get the information elsewhere. Remember, it is not just your ability to teach information; it is perspective and personality that differentiates you.

While value-driven content in the three areas we discussed above is at the forefront of a smart strategy, the good news is delivering that content is not all on you. Some of the most influential strategic business leaders I know utilize their platform to turn the spotlight on others. When you involve others in your content, you open up exposure to their audiences as well—whether including their story in a contributed article for a media outlet like *Fast Company*, tagging them on LinkedIn, interviewing them on your podcast, or simply reposting their work to congratulate them on their latest honor. Featuring others in your content allows you to foster goodwill and provide a win-win interaction. Not only do they appreciate being included, but they are also more likely to share, engage with, and amplify the content. This can be a powerful way to broaden your network online and off. This tactic can be practiced with your customers, potential prospects, peers, investors, and employees. A mindset shift I encourage you to consider is the more people you involve in your content, the more valuable and impactful it will become to your audience. It is a similar mindset to the type of talent you want to hire as a leader. Your perceived value increases with those you include in your content.

Hopefully this gives you a sense of relief and excites you to start thinking about the people and organizations you want to feature. When done correctly, content marketing should drive a portion of your business development. At the end of the day, both are focused on relationship-building and establishing trust. Mastering the blend of business development and content allows you to make the most impactful use of your time.

Step 6

TURBOCHARGE YOUR REFERRALS

S mall businesses are the backbone of the US economy, employing almost half of the workforce and representing 43.5% of the country's GDP.[1] In truth, helping small businesses succeed is why I decided to write this book—they make a positive impact across every fabric of our society, and it is getting harder and harder for them to compete.

Entrepreneurs are not just running businesses; they are creating workplaces, supporting families, and driving change every day. Knowing the pivotal role small businesses play long-term for our society, we will dive deep in this chapter on how to scale and future-proof the businesses we lead. The question is: How do we turbocharge growth with the right customer base?

Many leaders have a similar story to Sara Blakely of SPANX when they started their business. Often, you launch a product or service with a $0 marketing budget, and the only way customers learn about your business at that time is through word-of-mouth, circles of influence, and good old-fashioned hustle. For a small business, this rings true as the business begins to grow because the resources are never there to compete with the large corporate brands that can pay for millions of impressions. Word-of-mouth tactics are as old as time, but they are still one of the most vital strategies for a business today, and I want to help you supercharge your referral marketing strategy in this chapter.

A survey conducted by customer relationship management system Constant Contact found that 82% of small businesses said their main source of new business is referrals.[2] This means the small businesses in this category have already mastered a proven service or product because people are willing to refer them repeatedly. Referred business also often results in warmer leads, decreased sales cycles, and longer customer lifetime values.[3] So it is vital to our businesses to capitalize on understanding how we get referrals and how to increase their volume and velocity for our business.

Let's first examine where referrals are generated. Word-of-mouth referrals typically come from one of three referral sources.

1. Satisfied customers (current or past)
2. Strategic partnerships
3. Offline and online network (friends, peers, family, classmates, etc.)

Satisfied customers are often at the top of the list for most small businesses. If your business receives the highest deal flow from this audience, I want to congratulate you. This category is the highest form of flattery for a leader because it affirms the quality of your product or service and how you care for your customers. You are creating an experience for your customers they ultimately want to go out and share. You can see referrals come from current or past customers—this is why the relationship-building content category I discussed in the last step is crucial to staying top of mind. I want you to examine how referrals are happening from customers. Most often, it's by pure happenstance. You have the right client, at the right networking event, standing at the right cocktail event, and what you do comes up, and the client inserts your name. You hope these instances happen often, but the reality is you have no control over when they happen. It can be a slower grind if you do not have a referral strategy to gain momentum as a business relying on this audience for most of your lead flow.

Strategic partnership referrals tend to be more intentional because they are often arranged with complementary businesses. One of the best strategies as a leader is to look at your industry landscape and find businesses or centers of influence with similar ideal client profiles and complementary, but not overlapping, products or services to build strategic partnerships with. This approach allows small businesses, often B2B businesses, to surround their customers with an encompassing ecosystem, ultimately increasing their group's perceived value. A strong relationship with partnership businesses allows you to get clarity on how you might work together to serve one client and understand what makes a good client for one another. To be successful, this strategy requires alignment on customer service, ideal client profile, and company values. For example, our PR and marketing agency, Zilker Media, does a full suite of marketing services but does not provide in-house website design and development for our clients. This was an important, strategic decision for our firm, and we wanted our clients to have their websites produced by a specialty firm because we understood the complexities of these projects. So our team forged trusted, strategic partners to recommend to our clients. When we make a recommendation, that referral comes in warmer to a sales cycle because we shared how much experience we have had working with the other firm in the past. This knowledge accelerates the speed of trust in the minds of our clients. The goal of building strategic partnerships is to create a repeated all-around winning experience for you, your partners, and your clients. The confidence and trust factor must be built between strategic partners on the quality of the product or service a client will receive. If not, it can come back on the referring partner and negatively impact their business. While the risk with this strategy can be substantial, the rewards are high with the right partners.

The last audience we typically see referrals from are your general networks. This can include those you are connected with through online platforms and off. This referral audience, like the first one, is mostly driven by happenstance occurrences. An old colleague could see a LinkedIn post from you on their feed and be reminded to share your name with their neighbor needing a new CPA. A parent from the PTA remembered your business contributed to the latest fundraiser and knew her cousin was looking for a new physician. This audience might not have experienced your product or service, but they know and trust you. As your network expands, your referrals to this audience will grow over time, but you will have no control over the velocity of this growth without a strategy to turbocharge it.

WHAT DRIVES WORD-OF-MOUTH REFERRALS

To successfully boost referred business, we must understand what drives referrals—or, better yet, why people refer business in the first place. The science of why people refer products and services boils down to basic human behaviors and psychological drivers. It is unsurprising that referrals are just as much about the person making the recommendation as they are about the prospect receiving it. The driver for a referral is simple—they want to help out a friend. The personal gratitude people get when they provide that recommendation to a friend is centered around three desires:

- To make an impact
- To be seen as an authority
- To enhance reputation

I believe referrals stem from people's desire to do good for their friends, family, and community. It is meaningful when you can help a peer achieve a dream or solve a problem by sharing the best solution. The instant gratification you feel when you are a part of what has been accomplished is rewarding.

Some people with vast networks like the perception of being seen as someone who can offer a valuable recommendation. Take the process of applying to a private school for your kids as an example. Sure, anyone can technically apply to the school. But we all know that if you are "in the know" with someone in the school or on the school board, you can jump the ridiculous waiting list and get a meeting with the headmaster. Private schools drive referral demand because the families involved love to share with everyone how rarely they accept new students, even convincing parents they need to put their children on the waiting list. How that works, I really have no idea! Once parents hear about the low acceptance rate, the desire to be part of that school grows, no matter if the academics truly are the best in town. The same happens when we are able to name-drop leaders and companies we are connected with; it can give us a leg up on our social status if there is a high perceived value in our affiliation. Do you have that friend who is always getting into the latest trendy restaurant in town or telling you about their trip to a hidden speakeasy they got on the list for? They want to be known as the go-to source and love the feeling of having the access desired by their circles of influence.

Lastly, the desire to enhance reputation applies to every referral source. Your reputation is the foundation of your life. When you make a referral, you put your stamp of approval on it, so it is important that it remains an impressive, positive experience for the individual you have referred. Each successful referral experience not only benefits the recipient but also elevates you. It is a prideful experience when our friends are impressed by something we gave them access to. At the end of the day, we simply want the businesses or products we refer to make us look good in our networks. The more they do, the more we want to refer them.

This means that we, as leaders, must build brands people want to associate with in social and business settings. Your goal is to create a brand that is not only rewarding for your customers and team but also for your referral partners. The more we keep this in mind, the more we will see our audiences of influence look for opportunities to send prospects our way. This type of brand affinity can be driven when referral sources are armed with strong assets to share, feel a sense of excitement around the brand, or have received high perceived value from you in the past.

When a referral is made, the individual who has just been given your information is not going to drive to your store, email you, or give you a call first. The first thing they will do is google your name to learn more about their friend's recommendation before they make that first touchpoint. Although they come to you with perceived trust built by their friend, that can all crumble if what they find online when they google your name does not align with what their friend said about you. This is why the first three steps in this book are so crucial. You must get your image and first impression right to get prospects, investors, or potential employees to take the next step. This evaluation is critical for not only your corporate brand but also your brand as a Strategic Business Influencer. Especially if you are a B2B service business, referrals are often driven by your name versus your company's name. Remember, you represent your business just as much online as offline. If you have not taken the time to find clarity on how to share your brand, determine if you are differentiated, and examine the impact your first impression has; you can drive all the top-of-the-funnel activity you want, but at the end of the day, it will not convert.

While you evaluate your online assets, determine if this is an asset a referral source would be eager to share with their network. Your website hero image should, at first glance, provide a wow factor for your referral sources by showcasing your credibility and differentiation through visuals such as photos of you giving a keynote onstage or media logos of where your business has been featured. It might be a valuable lead magnet assessment you create, like Lisa Sun's Confidence Language quiz, that starts the conversation off with personalized feedback for the referral. Maybe it is a *Forbes* article you were interviewed for that is shared with the prospect. You want to arm your referral sources with assets that drive an exclusive, high perceived value to make them look good. It's imperative to ensure all of the assets someone can find of you online reinforce their recommendation.

Your time, energy, and resources are better spent getting your foundation right and understanding how to leverage your assets in your strategy to drive referrals. The reality is that a corporate marketing campaign you put out on social media or email will not have as high a conversion rate as word-of-mouth referrals made by trusted sources. That is because people trust people over logos—proving why the social media influencer market has now reached over $24 billion, according to Statista.[4] Also, avoid resorting to the traditional corporate marketing tactics of referral discount programs. It might incentivize a current customer to drive recommendations in the short term, but it does not build referral behavior or a premium they are excited to talk about long-term. Good referral sources want to act as your trusted gatekeepers, and it is in your best interest to let them take on that role. It will only increase your deal flow and perceived value.

GET INTENTIONAL WITH YOUR REFERRAL NETWORK

Utilizing your content strategy as a reason to reach out and engage your referral sources is where your marketing and lead generation strategy meet. As a small business leader, you must scrutinize every marketing activity you pour time and resources into to maximize impact and minimize budget. Remember, content is not about just providing information; you are helping your audience navigate whichever industry you are an expert in. Bringing in outside resources to help you do this only enhances your credibility to your audience. Weaving your business development process into your content strategy allows you to fill your top-of-the-funnel activity and expedite your sales cycles. Creative, useful, insightful, and distinctive content is the path to mutually beneficial relationships and enthusiastic referrals to new audiences. So, let's take a look at how you can start implementing this for your business. Now that you have identified your referral sources and why they refer you, the next step is to get tactical on who in your network you want to empower to talk about you. As a small business leader, it is easy to get caught up in the traditional approach to business development. Most businesses continue to approach sales and relationship-building the same way it has been done for the past several decades. They are blasting the typical "let's grab lunch / coffee / drinks / insert activity here" email or the "I'm in town this week, I would love to catch up" to their prospects or referral sources. With this approach, it is harder to get a "yes" response because you are fighting with everyone else for those time slots with the same ask. It also sets up the impression you are about to ask them for a favor or put them into a sales conversation before you even have an opportunity to open your mouth. This understanding from that outreach alone will cause most people to delete your email without a response. This type of outreach approach also hinders the amount of ground you can cover to the number of coffees, lunches, and dinners you can have in a week. If you are not physically in front of someone when you get the "yes," you are not top of mind. This cold email blast tactic has you firing on all cylinders with no aim and provides no differentiation for your business.

Although there is nothing wrong with pursuing business development meetings, the reality is leaders only have so many hours in a day and so many days in a week. The referral strategy for Strategic Business Influencers takes a bit of an opposite approach. It avoids falling into the expensive and slow-churning cold lead generation trap. Instead, the Strategic Business Influencer approach focuses on tapping into your existing relationships to spin off and accelerate high-quality leads while creating interactions that people want to discuss with their network.

To have an effective referral strategy, keep your relationship-building efforts microtargeted. The success of referral marketing is not a numbers game; it is measured by the depth of connection you can build with someone over time. This dovetails with the approach we just walked through with PR, social media, and building an audience you own. I want you to start by creating a list of 25 to 35 names you want to empower, deepen, or build relationships with over the next 12 to 18 months. These names should be those you believe have access and exposure to the right, ideal client profile for you. I imagine if you are an entrepreneur reading this book you probably already have names coming to mind that you need to write down. I typically recommend keeping this list of names in an Excel spreadsheet or customer relationship management system like HubSpot to allow for easy segmenting. This exercise should be done alongside your sales team, if you have one, as part of your business development plan. Once the names are listed, bucket them into referral source groups to identify if they are a customer, partner, or network connection. This will help you ensure you are balancing your referral network across all three areas. The goal is not to reach out to each of the 35 names asking for a sales conversation. I want you to use the assets you have built as a Strategic Business Influencer as a reason to reach out and connect. This approach will put you in a dynamic two-way interaction versus a traditional one-way sales interaction. Offering useful, insightful, distinctive content is the path to mutually beneficial relationships and enthusiastic referrals to new audiences. So, what exactly do you do with this list of names to start the process? You have four potential reasons you can approach each person on your list.

- Interview them on your platform.
- Utilize them as a source for press.
- Involve them in an interactive campaign.
- Gift them something they want to share.

Guest Spotlight Series

It's time to put your media hat on and start an interview series on your platform. When you do this, you become the media host or journalist and sit in the production seat. The power of an interview series is that the tables are turned in a conversation. It is your job to ask good questions and learn more about their business, personal life, challenges, and triumphs. Does this task sound familiar to you? It should be what you are already doing in your business development conversations.

To create your interview series, think of a theme that represents a commonality in your industry. For example, a local commercial architecture firm does not necessarily have to create an interview series on the topic of different architectural styles. Their audience as a commercial firm isn't fellow architects who would find that information fascinating; it is referral partners like general contractors or developers. With this niche target audience in mind, create a topic you and your target guests could discuss in a two-way conversation. This could be an interview series called "BuiltATX," discussing the demands of the city and how the commercial construction industry is working together to meet them. Or "Built on Sustainability," featuring the top local general contractors and developers who are changing the landscape to better the community. Whatever the topic might be, home in on a theme you believe your guests will be passionate about and offer plenty of opportunities for them to showcase their expertise.

A guest spotlight series can be as high or low production as you would like. What is most important is that you are getting the time you need in front of your prospect or referral source. Your series can be written, audio-only, or video format. A written format is typically the most productive and least time-consuming approach. With a written interview series, you send your five to seven interview questions over email for the guest to answer in their own time and return to you. Once they have submitted their answers, you can add their biography, headshot, and a written introduction to post the interview in its entirety on your website or LinkedIn channel, tagging the guest.

One commercial broker of a global firm did exactly this on his LinkedIn page to propel relationship-building and word-of-mouth referrals in the toughest commercial real estate environment we have seen in the last couple of decades. Instead of just competing for business by relying on his entertainment budget, he added a differentiating experience for prospects by featuring them on his platform. He had the top executives all posting about him on LinkedIn through this strategy.

My recommendation with this format is to interview the guest over the phone if you can to craft the written interview. This creates a more personable experience for the time and effort you put into the series. An audio-only format can be produced as a podcast and can be distributed on one or many channels. This does require extra money and time in setting up and production, but it does provide an opportunity for a live 30- to 45-minute conversion. You can buy podcasting equipment and conduct the interviews in person, or you can conduct them with your earphones through Zoom. Video interviews also have the flexibility to be conducted in person or on Zoom. In fact, a lot of podcasts are now also videocasts because of the accessibility Zoom has given us. The opportunity audio and video give us that email does not is the rapport building that happens before the recording begins and after. If you are in-person recording and have a physical office you bring guests to, you also have an opportunity to create an experience out of the interview.

I introduced you to Jeff Wilkinson, chairman and CEO of Keystone Bank, in the introduction of this book. Before starting Keystone Bank, Jeff had been a serial entrepreneur and leader in the banking industry for years. Because Jeff built up a strong reputation and decades of valuable relationships in his network, he was able to leverage this clout to start Keystone Bank. He knew that, with Austin's growing entrepreneurial scene, building a bank with the vision to be the best bank in town for local entrepreneurs would still be a challenging feat because, with this target audience, Keystone Bank would be going directly up against the big global banks with a local presence. Most bankers in town were building relationships the old-fashioned way I mentioned earlier. They were attending the networking events, sponsoring entrepreneurial events in town, and asking for all of the coffees, lunches, and dinners. Jeff, an entrepreneur himself, knew that entrepreneurs valued trusted credibility, a customized experience, and an accessible relationship with decision-makers. The latter two desires were challenging for big banks to provide. He sought for Keystone to take a unique approach to relationship-building that had never been seen before in the banking industry. Keystone Bank leveraged both a spotlight series and award-driven PR to create that differentiation. They started a video podcast called *Banking on Community* hosted by Jeff that was filmed in their downtown branch podcast studio. The subject of the podcast was not the latest trends entrepreneurs should know about banking or some other industry-specific subject. The theme of the podcast was local leaders sharing their stories and the impact they have made on the community. A simple topic that focused entirely on the guest.

Their team created a list of relationships that included clients, network contacts, partnerships, and team members they wanted to elevate profiles for. Instead of emailing each contact to ask for the typical happy-hour meetup, they emailed each other, inviting them to be a guest on Jeff's podcast. With Jeff's reputation he had built over the years, this was seen as an honor for many entrepreneurs to sit down with him and have an opportunity to share their stories.

To increase your likelihood of receiving a "yes" when crafting this type of outreach to guests, convey why you believe they would be a great fit for the series and what the interview will highlight about them. Think about it as a way to show authentic admiration and build goodwill from the start. In Keystone's case, the outreach email looked something like this:

Subject line: Interview Invitation to Join Jeff Wilkinson's Podcast

Hi David,

I hope you are well.

Our chairman & CEO, Jeff Wilkinson, mentioned your name when discussing the top leaders in Austin who are making a difference in our city. He is a raving fan of what you have built with Zilker Securities.

My name is Nichole and I am coordinating Jeff Wilkinson's podcast, *Banking on Community*. He would love to have you as a guest so we can feature your story and the impact you are making in the community. You can see previous episodes **linked here**! Previous guests include the mayor, bestselling authors, and award-winning local entrepreneurs. We would love to have you join this esteemed guest list.

This interview would take place in Keystone Bank's very own podcast studio with audio and video at their branch location in downtown Austin!

Our team will craft the questions to guide the conversation, which you will receive ahead of time as well. If you are up for sitting down with Jeff, could you send back some availability in April? I will coordinate with Jeff and find a time for us to book.

We look forward to hearing from you and please don't hesitate to reach out if you have any questions at all. Always happy to help!

All the best,

Nichole

The magic in this outreach is you have just accelerated the ability to create a direct line of communication to the most powerful external influencer for your business, the decision-maker. Let's break down why.

With traditional outreach, your sales team might have taken weeks or months to get past gatekeepers to reach this level of access. Since you are now considered "the media" in the guest's eyes, this type of subject line will elicit an email open and a quicker response than a typical business development ask. This perception from your guests will create a distinct transition in their minds that will only build your influence as a business leader. Leading with an interview inquiry will catch the attention of your decision-maker, provide a sense of flattery, and avoid being passed downstream to a junior team member. By including in your note past guests and a link to past episodes, you build credibility for outreach to decision-makers that are not as familiar with you.

No matter the format, there are a few dos and don'ts to follow when creating your interview series.

Do invest your time in leading the interview series. Every word of this book is about focusing your time as a leader on the most impactful marketing activities that will support your business. Relationship-building is a top priority on that short list we have walked through in each chapter. The ability to use your influence to get your foot in the door and act as an accelerant for your business will considerably drive results. This does not mean you cannot bring in other key leaders in your business to fulfill part of the hosting duties—especially if they are publicly representing your business in a client-facing capacity. In fact, I encourage you to bring others on your team in to build their brands as Strategic Business Influencers. But this is not an activity you should completely take a back seat on. If you do, you only limit the results this effort can generate.

Do not get caught up in vanity metrics. Avoid defaulting your attention to traditional marketing metrics you might have learned in the past to measure an interview's success. The number of episode listeners, engagements, or followers does not adequately measure the business results you will see from the interviews. You are utilizing the interviews to fuel your pipeline, referrals, and business development process. That is the return for the resources and time you invest in doing this.

Do tag your interview guests when you post the interview. The best way to drive referrals is by giving the people in your network a reason to talk about you in a way that makes them look good. The interview series provides an opportunity for guests to do exactly that. When the interview is published on your website or social media channels (more about that below), tag the guest and the company individually. Make it as easy as possible for your guests to share the interview with their network—remember, it is an inadvertent way they can talk about themselves. When guests do this, it multiplies your network to their audience of like-minded decision-makers. You also are ingrained for a good while as a top-of-mind referral for anyone they come in contact with seeking out your products or services.

Do not make this a sales pitch. One of the quickest ways to kill the results you will see from an interview series is by making the interview interaction about you. If a relationship is established on trust and credibility, a prospect inquiry or referral from them will come with time. Use this interview as an opportunity to connect with your guest on a deeper level and showcase the value you bring as a Strategic Business Influencer to the conversation.

Do make this a cornerstone of your online content. Upcycle your interview series to drive content for your corporate and personal assets. The interview series should live on a landing page of your website and your social media channels and be featured in your newsletter content. The guests you bring on and the conversations that develop will not only deliver meaningful relationships for your business; it will also provide valuable content for your audience. Maximize the value of your interview series by killing two birds with one stone and setting it up to drive the content you are putting out for your audience to stay top of mind.

Associating yourself with key decision-makers will only increase credibility with your audience.

Expert Source Feature

Similar to the guest spotlight interview series, reaching out to interview a leader for a feature in an article you are writing for *Fast Company* shifts the perception of the engagement from business development to influential media members. As you start to master the tactics in step 4 to generate targeted press for your business, look for ways to include those on your relationship-building list in a meaningful interaction. A press feature is a memorable exchange and arms that decision-maker with a reason to talk about you to others, keeping you top of mind. Leaders will see this opportunity as a win for themselves and their business.

Interactive Campaigns

When launching an exclusive female executive online community, one bold leader had the idea of utilizing her inner network of entrepreneurs to create a hush-hush, grassroots-style approach. Her goal was to create demand for a high-end community membership without ever having to personally sell the community brand or benefits. She was launching this as a new passion venture outside of her primary business. She armed her small but mighty list of inner-circle relationships with a 90-day challenge they would all participate in on LinkedIn that focused on empowering wealth, business, personal relationships, and wellness for women. She coordinated the activation through email and included specific topics for group members to post about each week. These directives allowed her inner circle to speak to the core pillars of the group while personalizing the message. The only "branding" part of the campaign was the hashtag included on each post. With this coordinated strategy, she was able to rally over 1,000 members of women executives in a matter of weeks. Is there an interactive campaign you can rally your inner circle around to talk about your message in a personalized way? Think of it as a traditional grassroots strategy on steroids.

A Gift Worth a Post

You have probably read about the power of gifting to increase referrals when done right by thought leaders like the late John Ruhlin, who wrote the best book on the topic, *Giftology*. To add another layer to this never-failing strategy, give a gift that is worth a share. It might not be shared every time, but more often than not, this strategy works. We stumbled upon this strategy after seeing its effectiveness with our own agency business. For decades we have worked alongside bestselling business and healthcare authors to launch their books. There was a cookie shop in town that was the first of its kind and had been all over the media (another important win for PR!) that custom-printed photos on cookies at events. After seeing those news stories, an idea was born. We started shipping clients around the nation cookies with their book covers printed on them to congratulate their work the week of the launch. We did not anticipate this, but we found that clients couldn't share their custom cookies with their audiences fast enough on social media. The cookies gave them another way to plug their book but also gave them a reason to tag our company page and team's personal profile to talk about their experience working with us. Throughout the years, we have seen referral introductions and inquiries come in because they saw that their trusted peer worked with our team.

THE POWER OF YOUR CIRCLES OF INFLUENCE

Where a lot of small business owners spin their wheels is putting all their time and money into traditional advertising campaigns that pay for cold impressions. Paid impressions only result in high costs, longer sales cycles, and a gamble on whether you will receive a return on investment because the trust has not been established, and the perceived value simply is not there yet. To circumvent this vicious cycle that can prevent scalability for small businesses, start small by activating who you know. Your existing relationships and acquaintances are powerful, low-cost, yet high-return assets. When you empower your circles of influence with the right reason to talk about your business, you create a ripple effect of:

- Quality referrals
- Valuable content for your audience
- Goodwill for your relationships
- Expedited trust with those who do not know you yet

Just as you approach relationship-building in other aspects of your life, some of these results do not happen overnight. But with intentionality, this influence-driven strategy has the ability to scale quickly over time for your business. You are not boiling the ocean here—you are maximizing the time and effort you have already invested, focusing exactly where your leadership makes the greatest impact.

Conclusion

YOUR MOST IMPORTANT METRIC

With technology, the ability to have instant gratification, and information overload, you might feel like the speed of life is getting faster.

The pressure on leaders to keep up with the quickening pace of change is crucial to decreasing their risk of marginalization. *Harvard Business Review* analyzed that speed is not only crucial for top-line growth; it's equally important to "play defense" and create a true strategic advantage.[1] Alongside this, audiences are demanding that trust be built faster. In today's marketplace, the speed-to-trust metric is the most crucial metric you can control as a leader. Your reputation, experiences, and relationships are already your most valuable assets. It is time to leverage them fully to build a competitive advantage that matters—and lasts.

Becoming a Strategic Business Influencer is no longer a luxury in your strategy; it is a must-have to build a hedge strategy for today's marketplace competition. Putting this strategy into practice will not only drive business results; it will bring amplification to your mission and establish your legacy. Finding true fulfillment is what ignited the flame and fueled the fire for the stories of the Strategic Business Influencers featured in this book. As you evaluate your first impression, establish your Influence ID, and create ownership of your audience through the right PR, content, and referrals, I encourage you to stay true to what I call the four rules of influence:

1. It is a marathon, not a sprint.
2. You cannot automate you.
3. Never give up your brand equity.
4. Only be you.

I know it is ironic to ask entrepreneurs to follow the rules, but hey, they are here to keep you centered on what will drive fulfillment every day—achieving your mission.

RULE ONE: IT IS A MARATHON, NOT A SPRINT

Like many overnight success stories, the sentiment that long-lasting brands are built overnight is never true. I encourage you to be wary of any quick hack or tactic promising results from just content activity or press opportunities without weaving the other influence steps to create a long-term strategy. There is no shortcut to building your brand as a Strategic Business Influencer—nor would you want one. Influence is relationship-driven, not transactional. The entrepreneurs in this book focused on building and maintaining trust over time rather than viral, quick wins. The value of your brand is not in the visibility of the moment; it is in how you leverage that opportunity over time to scale your ability as a leader. Look for opportunities to reinforce the right exposure to influence your business development process, growth of an audience you own, and set up for the next venture. Half the battle for leaders is finding a path to sustainable growth. As you implement each step, analyze what you do behind the scenes daily that could scale with the right visibility. Approaching your brand with this mindset will ease the consistency required for longevity.

Your brand as an entrepreneur will always be dynamic as you create new spokes on your wheel and it gains traction through life. Avoid becoming paralyzed by needed change or the vision for change. Instead, I encourage you to utilize change as the catalyst to begin this journey. Building a strong foundation now will serve as a springboard for future ventures, board seats, and new roles in life. Treating your brand like a marathon will avoid having to stop and start your new initiatives from ground zero every time. Unlike one-hit internet influencers, your value is in meaningful, high-touch relationships over the sheer number of eyeballs.

RULE TWO: YOU CANNOT AUTOMATE YOU

Your brand is not a set it and forget it strategy. The six steps to influence require integration and insight into your daily responsibilities that move the needle for your business. Setting automated tactics like auto LinkedIn messaging campaigns to book discovery calls or buying cold lists to email blasts, even if it is from "you," are outdated tactics that require volume in resources and provide mediocre results. While there can be aspects of the process in each of the six steps that can be integrated with automation, the competitive advantage of this strategy centers around not being able to replicate you.

Marketing automation has leveled the playing field for companies, creating an environment where it is now challenging to establish differentiation. With access to automated content creation and marketing workflows, everyone can push a high content volume in front of audiences. It is no longer enough to get content in front of your audience at the right time because of this. Audiences are starting to see through automation workflows and become more selective of the content they consume. Because of this, I encourage you to lean into the aspects of your leadership that cannot be replicated. Remember, trust is personal and cannot be programmed. Focusing on bringing the right visibility to these areas will beat out machine automation any day. Keep your time and resources centered on building authentic, meaningful interactions versus mass production. Automatic algorithms can support speeding up content deployment, but they cannot replicate personal experiences and industry insight. At the heart of a Strategic Business Influencer strategy are high-touch relationships. Automation can support surface-level communication but falls short of creating trust-based connections. Stay above the noise by not falling victim to automated thought leadership.

RULE THREE: NEVER GIVE UP YOUR BRAND EQUITY

What I am most passionate about is leaders fully owning control of their brand online. Control takes an offensive approach by leaders that requires a good amount of groundwork, which we discussed in the first three steps. However, being proactive in establishing a strong foundation pays dividends in the long run. It is heartbreaking to think of leaders who have spent decades building a meaningful business to watch their reputation crumble overnight due to lack of ownership, allowing someone else to control the narrative. Whether it is an acquisition, crisis situation, or strategic decision, controlling the impression and message is crucial to the outcomes we face as business leaders.

Do not mistake intentionally avoiding an online presence as strategic. The impact is not only limiting for your business, but it is also opening your reputation and everything you have worked for to a high amount of risk. It is mission-critical for leaders to maintain control of their brand to influence future leads, partnerships, talent acquisition, investors, and the launch of new ventures. Think of the time you put into building your brand as a Strategic Business Influencer as an investment that will compound over time when executed with intentionality. Fully owning your brand online is the most valuable investment you can make in today's environment.

RULE FOUR: ONLY BE YOU

It is a simple yet challenging rule for leaders. I hear many entrepreneurs say, "What do I have to say that will be profound?" We tend to put our attention and worry on the messenger rather than the impactful message. I encourage you to channel your mindset on relentlessly getting your mission and message out there. Your job is to solely be the messenger, not the center of the message. So, there should be no pressure to become a certain persona.

Trying to emulate someone you are not will only lead to burnout. You will struggle to find enjoyment and fulfillment in being a Strategic Business Influencer because your approach is inauthentic. To be impactful, lean into what makes you a strong leader. This might be educating, writing, casting vision, or speaking—it will be different for everyone. The beauty of being a Strategic Business Influencer is that it is rooted in what you naturally excel at. People are craving the authenticity only other, real people can bring in a filtered, machine-driven online world. Your top priority is to convey what makes you and your company valuable in a way that showcases your strengths to reinforce why someone should trust and believe in you. Staying authentic in your approach will keep your efforts not only driving results for your business but personally rewarding long term.

Architecting your brand as a Strategic Business Influencer will look different for everyone, depending on your mission, what you enjoy doing, and your goals. That is why this strategy is effective, no matter the individual, company, or industry. As you begin the journey of building your brand as a Strategic Business Influencer, I want you to stop and ask yourself the question I asked the room of 12 entrepreneurs. It is now the question I ask every leader I meet.

Who are you in addition to being an entrepreneur?

Your answer is the power of your influence to make an impact on others (and your business).

ACKNOWLEDGMENTS

To my husband, Jordan—thank you for being a true partner and the best dad. Your belief in me, especially on the days I couldn't find it myself, has meant everything. Thank you for reading every word of the early drafts of this book—even when reading isn't your favorite hobby. Your steady, unwavering support has carried me more times than you know.

To my son, Landry—this manuscript came to life during your first year, from two months to one year postpartum. It was one of the most challenging and inspiring seasons of my life. I'm so grateful to be your mom, and even more grateful to have documented this journey in a way that you'll one day hold in your hands.

To my parents, Cristina and Mark—you've taken every phone call, made countless sacrifices, and driven hours just to show up. I'll never be able to repay that. I only hope I can be half as great a parent as you've been to me. I'm forever grateful for the way you continue to support me and my family so I can always pursue my dreams.

To Granna and Grandpa (the smartest man in the world)—thank you for helping me dream bigger, for introducing me to my first creative outlet of music, for answering my countless questions about life, and for showing up to every event, always cheering Halen and me on.

To Doodle and Marsha—thank you for your unconditional love and support. For the endless rounds of "stage introductions" as I ran into the room as a little girl, for nurturing my love of music, and for walking beside me like second parents through so many seasons of life. Your entrepreneurial ventures continue to inspire me deeply.

To my brother, Halen—thank you for the countless ways you've supported me throughout my life. I admire your work ethic, your character, and the steady presence you bring to our family. I'm proud to call you my brother. To my sister-in-law, Hailey—thank you for your love, your laughter, and your unwavering support. I'm so grateful for the relationship we share.

To Rusty and Paige—thank you for your partnership, your mentorship, and the opportunity to build Zilker Media together. Rusty, this book would not exist without you. Thank you for being in it with me word for word and encouraging me every step of the way.

To Matt Holt and Will Weisser—thank you for seeing the early vision of this book and giving me the opportunity to bring it to life for leaders who need it most.

To the Matt Holt Books team—thank you for your hard work, collaboration, and guidance. This book is better because of your shared vision.

To our Zilker Media leadership team—Shelby, Nichole, Haley, and Patti—what a gift it is to build this company alongside you. Your leadership, friendship, and hard work continue to inspire me.

To Clint Greenleaf—thank you for your mentorship and partnership at Zilker Media. I've learned so much from you about business and life, and I'm grateful for both.

To Melanie Cloth—thank you for being the creative force behind the images and assets for this book. Your genius shows up in every image, and I'm lucky to have your collaboration.

To the entire Zilker Media team—past and present—thank you for making the work not only possible but also meaningful (and fun). I learn from you every day, and I'm proud of the impact we create together.

To our Zilker Media clients—thank you for trusting us with your stories, your missions, and your vision. It's been an honor to partner with some of the world's most trusted leaders and companies. I'm continually inspired by the work you do, and I'm grateful for the opportunity to learn from you and create meaningful impact together.

To the Velasquez family—Tío Tony, Tía Monica, Tía Jennifer, Tía Laura, Tía Anabel—and to my amazing cousins: Thank you for the deep-rooted love and encouragement you've shown me over the years. Your support has meant more than you know.

To Pat and Tammy Budde—thank you for your constant love and support of both me and Jordan. I am so grateful to be part of this family.

To Chelsea, Tanner, Nic, Jackie, Ella, and Freddie—thank you for the love, laughs, and support. I'm so lucky to call you family. I can't wait to see the trails you kids blaze as you grow.

To Uncle Dan and Aunt Karen—thank you for your mentorship, your example of hard work and passionate entrepreneurship, and for what we lovingly call your "finishing school." We're all better because of it.

To the Davidsons—Cindy, Dave, and Nichole—thank you for being my second family. From taking me along to see the world, to modeling what it means to lead both a business and a family with strength and heart, your friendship and guidance have shaped me more than words can say. I'm forever grateful for the countless ways you've supported me.

To my EO Forum (Deuce Cinco)—Gordon, Nash, Emily, David, Brandon, Tenesha, Andies, and Marc—thank you for your encouragement, your challenges, and your reminders that mindset truly matters.

To my WPO Forum and Elizabeth Davis—this project wouldn't have been possible without your encouragement. I'm so grateful to be among such a powerhouse group of women.

To my C12 Forum and Michael Heflin—thank you for the wisdom shared at the table and for teaching me what it means to use business as a ministry.

To my first professional mentor, Shelby Sledge—you made a lasting impact on my life and career, and I'm forever thankful.

To Mr. Jones—my first leadership mentor—thank you for encouraging me to step into leadership and for instilling the values that still guide me today. Your reminder to always serve others and "do the right thing" has been a compass throughout my journey. I still start every meeting with "good things" because of you.

And finally, to the entrepreneurs whose stories are featured throughout this book—it's an honor to share your journeys. Thank you to Jeff Wilkinson, Jack Aspenson, Joyce Durst, Sarah Dusek, Meg Gluth, Tammie Chang, Jason P. Carroll, Lisa Sun, and Chris Kirksey for trusting me with them. I hope your stories go on to inspire others the way you've inspired me.

NOTES

Introduction: The Rise of the Strategic Business Influencer

1   SPANX, "About Us," About SPANX LLC Page, 2024, https://spanx.com /pages/about-us.

2   US Small Business Administration, "Frequently Asked Questions About Small Business, 2023," US Small Business Administration Office of Advocacy FAQ Page, March 7, 2023, https://advocacy.sba.gov/2023/03/07/frequently-asked-questions-about-small-business-2023/.

3   Bryan Reesman, "Who Is Zach Bryan, and How Did He Shoot to Fame?" *American Songwriter*, November 7, 2023, https://americansongwriter.com/who -is-zach-bryan-and-how-did-he-shoot-to-fame/.

4   Interview with Megan Gluth, 2024.

5   Megan Sauer, "Bumble CEO: Here Are the 'Crazy Hacks' I Used to Grow My App into a $1.9 Billion Company—One of Them Cost Only $20," *CNBC Make It*, October 15, 2023, https://www.cnbc.com/2023/10/15/whitney-wolfe -herd-i-grew-bumble-with-crazy-hacks-marketing-tactics.html.

6   Korn Ferry, "Workforce 2024 Global Insights Report," Korn Ferry Insights Page, 2024, https://www.kornferry.com/insights/featured-topics/workforce -management/workforce-planning-insights.

7   Roger Dooley, "What Is a Chief Executive Officer? CEO Role Explained,"

Forbes, April 21, 2024, https://www.forbes.com/sites/rogerdooley/article/chief
-executive-officer-ceo/.

8   Dooley, "What Is a Chief Executive Officer? CEO Role Explained."

9   Trainual, "Chief Executive Officer (CEO) Role and Responsibilities,"
Trainual the Manual Page, October 9, 2024, https://trainual.com/template
/chief-executive-officer-ceo.

10   A. G. Lafley, "What Only the CEO Can Do," *Harvard Business Review*, May
2009, https://hbr.org/2009/05/what-only-the-ceo-can-do.

11   Harry Hertz, "2024's CEO Challenge: Implement a Systems Perspective by
Accelerating the Speed of Trust," NIST, September 17, 2024, https://www
.nist.gov/blogs/blogrige/2024s-ceo-challenge-implement-systems-perspective
-accelerating-speed-trust#:~:text=Some%20Summary%20Thoughts,the%20
road%20to%20performance%20excellence!.

12   Edelman Trust Institute, "2024 Edelman Trust Barometer Global Report,"
Edelman, 2024, https://www.edelman.com/sites/g/files/aatuss191/files/2024-02
/2024%20Edelman%20Trust%20Barometer%20Global%20Report_FINAL.pdf.

13   Te-Ping Chen, "Gen Z Plumbers and Constructions Workers Are Making
#bluecollar Cool," *Wall Street Journal*, June 9, 2024, https://www.wsj.com
/lifestyle/careers/gen-z-plumbers-and-construction-workers-are-making
-bluecollar-cool-0c386274?reflink=share_mobilewebshare.

14   Interview with Jack Aspenson, 2024.

15   Interview with Joyce Durst, 2024.

Step 1: Create Your "Influence ID"

1   Brent Adamson and Nick Toman, "5 Ways the Future of B2B Buying Will
Rewrite the Rules of Effective Selling," The Gartner Website Sales Page,
August 4, 2020, https://emt.gartnerweb.com/ngw/globalassets/en/sales-service
/documents/trends/5-ways-the-future-of-b2b-buying.pdf.

2   Yuheng Li, Mladen Raković, Wei Dai, Jionghao Lin, Hassan Khosravi,
Kirsten Galbraith, Kayley Lyons, Dragan Gašević, and Guanliang Chen,
"Are Deeper Reflectors Better Goal-Setters? AI-Empowered Analytics of
Reflective Writing in Pharmaceutical Education," *Computers & Education:
Artificial Intelligence* 5 (2023): 100157, https://www.sciencedirect.com/science
/article/pii/S2666920X2300036X#se0140.

3   Gino Wickman, *Traction: Get a Grip on Your Business* (Dallas: BenBella Books, 2012).

4   Kim Schneiderman, "Writing as a Path to Self-Compassion," *Psychology Today*, January 1, 2022, https://www.psychologytoday.com/intl/blog/the-novel-perspective/202201/writing-as-a-path-to-self-compassion#:~:text=Writing%20about%20yourself%20in%20the,in%20a%20more%20positive%20light.

5   Alexandra Garfinkle, "90% of Online Content Could Be 'Generated by AI by 2025,' Expert Says," Yahoo! Finance, January 13, 2023, https://finance.yahoo.com/news/90-of-online-content-could-be-generated-by-ai-by-2025-expert-says-201023872.html.

6   Emily Yahr, "Bobby Bones, New to WMZQ, Hosts a Different Kind of Country Music Morning Radio Show," *Washington Post*, March 18, 2014, https://www.washingtonpost.com/entertainment/music/bobby-bones-new-to-wmzq-hosts-a-different-kind-of-country-music-morning-radio-show/2014/03/18/3d9fe638-aec5-11e3-9627-c65021d6d572_story.html.

Step 2: Evaluate Your First Impression

1   Rachel Greenwald, "A Matchmaker's Advice on How to Make a Great First Impression at Work," *Harvard Business Review*, January 5, 2021, https://hbr.org/2021/01/a-matchmakers-advice-on-how-to-make-a-great-first-impression-at-work.

2   Alexander Todorov, *Face Value: The Irresistible Influence of First Impressions* (Princeton, NJ: Princeton University Press, 2017).

3   William Standaert, Steve Muylle, Amit Basu, "Business Meetings in a Postpandemic World: When and How to Meet Virtually," *Business Horizons* 65 (2022): 267–75, doi: 10.1016/j.bushor.2021.02.047.

4   Abi Cook, Meg Thompson, and Paddy Ross, "Virtual First Impressions: Zoom Backgrounds Affect Judgements of Trust and Competence," *PLOS One* (2023): doi: 10.1371/journal.pone.0291444.

5   Gitte Lindgaard, Gary Fernandes, Cathy Dudek, and J. Brown, "Attention Web Designers: You Have 50 Milliseconds to Make a Good First Impression!" *Behaviour & Information Technology* 25, no. 2 (2006): 115–26, doi:10.1080/01449290500330448.

6   Jeffrey M. Jones, "Confidence in U.S. Institutions Down; Average at New

Low," Gallup, July, 5, 2002, https://news.gallup.com/poll/394283/confidence
-institutions-down-average-new-low.aspx.

7   PwC, "PwC's 2024 Trust Survey 8 Key Findings," The PwC Trust in US
    Business Survey Page, March 12, 2024, https://www.pwc.com/us/en/library
    /trust-in-business-survey.html.

8   Brian Dean, "Here's What We Learned About Organic Click Through Rate,"
    The Backlinko Google CTR Stats Page, November 1, 2024, https://backlinko
    .com/google-ctr-stats.

9   Interview with Chris Kirksey, February 2025.

10 Austin McCraw, "This Just Tested: Stock Images or Real People." Marketing
    Experiments, April 11, 2011, https://marketingexperiments.com/digital
    -advertising/stock-images-tested.

11 Interview with Megan Gluth, 2024.

12 Interview with Megan Gluth, 2024.

13 Interview with Megan Gluth, 2024.

14 Interview with Megan Gluth, 2024.

15 Tom Hedges, Tom, "AI in Search: Charting Changing Trends in Search
    Engines," GWI, August 14, 2024, https://blog.gwi.com/trends/ai-and-search/.

16 Gartner, "Gartner Predicts Search Engine Volume Will Drop 25% by 2026,
    Due to AI Chatbots and Other Virtual Agents," The Gartner Newsroom
    Page, February 9, 2024, https://www.gartner.com/en/newsroom/press-releases
    /2024-02-19-gartner-predicts-search-engine-volume-will-drop-25-percent-by
    -2026-due-to-ai-chatbots-and-other-virtual-agents.

17 Statista, "Number of Adults in the United States Using Generative Artificial
    Intelligence (AI) First for Online Search in 2023 and 2027," Statista Statistics
    Page, March 29, 2024, https://www.statista.com/statistics/1454204/united-
    states-generative-ai-primary-usage-online-search/#:~:text=In%202023%2C
    %20around%2013%20million,over%2090%20million%20online%20users.

Step 3: Build a Foundation for Audience Ownership

1   Trishla Ostwal, "Meta Beats Revenue Expectations Amid AI Push, but Ad
    Sales Growth Slows," Adweek, October 30, 2024, https://www.adweek.com
    /media/meta-beats-revenue-expectations-amid-ai-push-but-ad-sales-growth
    -slows/.

2   AppsFlyer, "AppsFlyer Data Reveals Increase in User Opt-In Rates and

Ad Spend on iOS Three Years After Apple's App Tracking Transparency,"
AppsFlyer Newsroom Page, April 26, 2024, https://www.appsflyer.com
/company/newsroom/pr/att-data-findings/.

3   Will Kenton, "Lead Magnet," Investopedia, January, 26, 2023, https://www
.investopedia.com/terms/l/lead-magnet.asp#:~:text=What%20Is%20a%20
Lead%20Magnet,magnets%20to%20create%20sales%20leads.

4   Klipfolio, "Email Newsletter Signup Conversion Rate," The Klipfolio
Resources Page, August 8, 2024, https://www.klipfolio.com/resources/kpi
-examples/digital-marketing/newsletter-signup-conversion-rate#:~:text=Email
%20Signup%20Conversion%20Rate%20Benchmark&text=Also%20known%20
as%20email%20capture,or%20more%20ECR%20is%20healthy.

5   Bob Sparkins, "High-Converting Lead Magnet Landing Pages: Examples,
Best Practices, and Templates," The Ultimate Guide to Lead Generation
Page, October 30, 2024, https://www.leadpages.com/lead-generation-guide
/lead-magnet-landing-page-examples.

6   Vibetrace, "Coupon Conversion Rate," The Vibetrace Blog Page, July 22,
2024, https://vibetrace.com/coupon-conversion-rate/?.

7   Cleveland Clinic News Service, "Why We Like Personality Quizzes,"
Cleveland Clinic, July 24, 2024, https://newsroom.clevelandclinic.org/2024
/07/24/why-we-like-personality-quizzes.

8   Dan Zarrella, "Which Types of Form Fields Lower Landing Page
Conversions?" The Hubspot Blog Page, June 11, 2021, https://blog.hubspot
.com/blog/tabid/6307/bid/6746/Which-Types-of-Form-Fields-Lower-Landing
-Page-Conversions.aspx.

Step 4: Create PR Buzz from Your Smartphone

1   Barbara Cave Henricks and Rusty Shelton, *Mastering the New Media Landscape:
Embrace the Micromedia Mindset* (Oakland: Berrett-Koehler Publishers, 2016).

2   Listen Notes, "Podcast Stats: How Many Podcasts Are There?" The Listen
Notes Podcast Stats page, October 18, 2024, https://www.listennotes.com
/podcast-stats/.

3   Interview with Jack Aspenson, 2024.

4   Interview with Joyce Durst, 2024.

5   Interview with Joyce Durst, 2024.

6   Interview with Joyce Durst, 2024.

Step 5: Develop Content That Drives Leads

1   Chris Walker, "Personal LinkedIn Profiles Outperform Company Pages with
    5x More Engagement," The Refine Labs News Page, April 26, 2023, https://
    www.refinelabs.com/news/personal-linkedin-engagement-vs-company
    -page#:˜:text=Posted%20by%20Chris%20Walker%20on,Bowen%2C%20
    President%20of%20Refine%20Labs.

2   Pew Research Center, "Social Media and News Fact Sheet," The Pew
    Research Center Journalism Page, September 17, 2024, https://www
    .pewresearch.org/journalism/fact-sheet/social-media-and-news-fact-sheet/.

3   AdEspresso, "Top Types of Images That Perform Well on Instagram in 2019,"
    AdEspresso, May 28, 2019, https://adespresso.com/blog/7-types-images
    -perform-well-instagram/.

4   Interview with Megan Gluth, 2024.

5   David Scott Meerman, "Newsjacking," The Newsjacking Home Page, June
    27, 2024, https://www.newsjacking.com/.

6   Gallup, "The Importance of Employee Recognition: Low Cost, High
    Impact," The Gallup Workplace Page, January 12, 2024, https://www.gallup
    .com/workplace/236441/employee-recognition-low-cost-high-impact.aspx.

7   Will Henshall, "4 Charts That Show Why AI Progress Is Unlikely to Slow
    Down," *TIME*, November 6, 2023, https://time.com/6300942/ai-progress
    -charts/.

Step 6: Turbocharge Your Referrals

1   Stephanie Ferguson Melhorn, Makinizi Hoover, and Isabella Lucy, "Small
    Business Center Data," US Chamber of Commerce Business Page, May 20,
    2024, https://www.uschamber.com/small-business/small-business-data-center.

2   Erica Tower, "Customer Engagement a Major Focus of Small Business
    Technology According to Constant Contact Technology Pulse Survey,"
    Constant Contact Press Release Page, August 16, 2024, https://news
    .constantcontact.com/press-release-customer-engagement-major-focus-small
    -business-technology-according-constant-contact-t.

3   Philipp Schmitt, Bernd Skiera, and Christophe Van den Bulte, "Why
    Customer Referrals Can Drive Stunning Profits," *Harvard Business Review*,
    June, 2011, https://hbr.org/2011/06/why-customer-referrals-can-drive
    -stunning-profits.

4   Statista, "Influencer Marketing Market Size Worldwide from 2016 to 2024," The Statista Marketing Page, February 6, 2024, https://www.statista.com /statistics/1092819/global-influencer-market-size/.

Conclusion: Your Most Important Metric

1   Suketu Gandhi, "What Fast-Moving Companies Do Differently," *Harvard Business Review*, October 18, 2023, https://hbr.org/2023/10/what-fast-moving -companies-do-differently.

ABOUT THE AUTHOR

Paige Velasquez Budde is a veteran marketer, entrepreneur, and keynote speaker.

She is a cofounding partner and the CEO of Zilker Media, an Austin-based agency that builds people-driven brands. During her tenure as CEO, the *Austin Business Journal* has named Zilker one of the city's fastest growing companies as well as one of its best places to work, two years in a row. It has also been listed on Austin Inno's list of "Coolest Companies."

Paige speaks about strategic business influence at many conferences and corporate events, including for organizations such as Ernst & Young, JPMorgan Chase, Harvard Medical School, the University of Texas at Austin, Camp Gladiator, Entrepreneurs Organization, and the Women Presidents Organization. She delivered a TEDx talk at the University of Texas Business School in March 2023. Her approach to people-driven marketing has been featured in media outlets such as *Inc.*, Thrive Global, KevinMD, *Texas CEO Magazine*, *Authority* magazine, Business News Daily, and Business.com.

Paige is a member of Women Presidents Organization, Entrepreneurs Organization, and C12. Paige has been named a finalist in the *Austin Business Journal*'s Women in Business awards and Austin Under 40 awards. She resides west of Austin in Dripping Springs, Texas, with her husband, Jordan; her son, Landry; and her dog, Spur.

READY to *activate* your STRATEGIC BUSINESS INFLUENCE?

DOWNLOAD THE INFLUENCE ID WORKBOOK

The workbook serves as a strategic identity guide for modern CEOs, entrepreneurs, and leaders looking to establish clarity, credibility, and consistency for their executive brand and company.

YOUR REPUTATION AS A LEADER IS YOUR MOST POWERFUL ASSET.

How effectively are you positioning your brand to accelerate trust and drive meaningful business results? Take the quiz and join the Strategic Business Influencer community for more resources at **paigevelasquezbudde.com**.